Dan Davies

ASPIRATION, IDENTITY
AND SELF-BELIEF
snapshots of social structure at work

D1382407

To Dan
with many thanks
and best wishes.
Richard
May 2010

ASPIRATION, IDENTITY
AND SELF-BELIEF
snapshots of social structure at work

Richard Riddell

Trentham Books

Stoke on Trent, UK and Sterling, USA

Winner of the IPG DIVERSITY Award 2010

Trentham Books Limited
Westview House   22883 Quicksilver Drive
734 London Road   Sterling
Oakhill   VA 20166-2012
Stoke on Trent   USA
Staffordshire
England ST4 5NP

First published 2010

British Library Cataloguing-in-Publication Data
A catalogue record for this book is available from the
British Library

ISBN: 978 1 85856 465 4

Designed and typeset by Trentham Books Ltd and
printed in Great Britain by Cpod, a division of the
Cromwell Group, Trowbridge, Wiltshire

Trentham is an ethical
publisher and uses paper
only from sustainable forests

CONTENTS

To my parents
Margaret (d. 2001) and Rodford (d. 2003)

Acknowledgements

I have many people to thank for the development of this book over four and a half years. First of all, my grateful thanks to the British Academy for making a rare small research grant award to an independent scholar such as myself. But at the same time, thanks to many staff in the School of Education at the University of the West of England, where I am a Visiting Fellow, am always made most welcome and where my fifty tapes were typed into the transcripts which formed the live evidence base for this book.

Most of all, deepest thanks to my colleague and friend, Professor David James, who not only read various versions of what I have been writing when he has had much better things to do, but took on the whole script of my first draft, all the time making helpful and perceptive comments ranging from phraseology to theory. David has helped guide me through the different way of thinking about the world of Bourdieusian sociology, something that I began to see the necessity of – without any previous background in sociology – soon after my last book came out. The cost of a few pints of real ale in various Good Beer Guide pubs in Bristol has seemed nugatory compared to the benefit.

I have also been guided in the process by Professor Stephen Ball, from the very early stages of forming a research proposal, and again by Professor Andrew Pollard. As I say in Chapter 1, I continue to be influenced in my own thinking by Andrew's view of the cyclical, iterative development of identity in flux, as a person moves from one social situation to another. Andrew was very encouraging as I first developed the notion of aspirational identity at the centre of this book. And thanks to these and other colleagues who listened to my presentations of three papers from this research at successive annual conferences of the British Education Research Association, and who gave me constructive and critical feedback.

Perhaps most of all I must thank the fifty plus individuals who agreed to be interviewed and taped and to provide the basis for my micro studies. In particular, the parents of children at the two independent schools – Deborah, Kate, Jenny, Ann, Geraldine, Adrian, Peter, Lynne, Fay, Kerry, and Charlotte, not their real names of course – who all spoke at length about their personal experiences, hopes and fears, without much prompting from me. The heads of the two schools, called Carter's and Merryweather in this book, made me most welcome and allowed me access to their staff.

I am grateful to the senior officials who also spoke openly – and anonymously of course – on tape and were able to give such a clear interpretation of the intentions of government policy. Although I only provide a direct quotation from one of them in the book, what they said guided me to the right documents and whom else to interview. In addition, through them, by putting my contact details on a departmental circular, I was able to speak to local Gifted and Talented Coordinators who were interested in the research. Thanks especially to Susan who read through what I wrote and agreed to be interviewed again.

I must thank all the staff at the former National Academy for Gifted and Talented Youth at Warwick University where I spent a few hours in 2006, unexpected by them! With another shake-up of Gifted and Talented provision being announced at the time this book was being finalised, this area of work is a showcase of the rapid forming and reforming of government policy.

Thanks to Terry, Malcolm, Veronica, Dianna, Celia and other staff working on admissions at the three universities I visited – and for feeding back so quickly on what I had written. And to Kevin, Lorna, Peter, Derek, Arthur and Donald who spoke with feeling and commitment about the needs of the most disengaged and needy members of our society. And to the five young people I interviewed in 2009 – Sally, Pat, Pete, Suze and Don – who brought this work alive and the need for it.

Finally, thanks once again to Rob Stokes, Deputy Editor at the *Bristol Evening Post*, for allowing us to use some of their school photos in the design of the book's cover, and most of all to Gillian at Trentham for her continued encouragement in the writing of this book and for helping me achieve clarity in what I have been trying to say.

Nevertheless, I alone am responsible for all the views, arguments and mistakes in this book.

Richard Riddell
Bristol, November 2009

1

How things in the UK stay
the way they are

When it's a notion
When it's still vague
It is praised.
When it looms big
When plans are in motion
Objections are raised.
Bertolt Brecht

Inequalities of circumstance

I do not come from an entirely privileged background. Although they raised me in a largish detached house in a prosperous suburb in south Manchester, my parents had little money after they had to sell the family business in the early 1960s. My father, after some spells out of work, resigned himself to a clerical job which diminished the standard of living we had enjoyed before. I remember that large winter electricity bills usually precipitated a family crisis and our house was a bit unkempt. And I was able to attend a highly selective grammar school, then direct grant, only thanks to a local authority scholarship, with my grandmother, a teacher, buying me a new blazer every two years.

These early experiences were no doubt formative of my later and current outlooks, but I am sure my sense of what is just and unjust began with my volunteering for the Manchester Youth and Community Service in my late teens. Several boys, as we still were, supervised by one of our masters, used to spend weekends decorating the homes of elderly people who lived in the communities round the school. Very often their home was a rented room in a decayed Victorian terrace, smelling of damp, with a few sticks of old decrepit furniture and lino flooring. A small (compared to us) elderly person who would make us tea. Invariably the landlord would appear to thank us. I don't know who provided the paint.

On one of these Saturdays, I was doing the preparation work for painting in a ground floor room in a house just round the corner from our school, overlooking a park. I was sealing cracks, seeing if we could block draughts and so on. There was what seemed to be a gale blowing in through a wooden cupboard under the window, screwed to the wall. Opening the cupboard, I found it open to the elements. It had no rear panel and behind it was a large hole in the front wall of the house, where bricks had obviously been removed at some time in the past and not replaced. The cupboard was stuffed with old newspapers which of course were damp. I remember the apologetic look on the elderly lady's face.

The UK in 2010

That experience was forty years ago. Yet in 2010 there remain profound inequalities of circumstance in the UK and, as I shall argue in this book, of opportunity.

In the late 1960s when I was decorating, and despite devaluation of the pound and IMF loans, the UK was still in the middle of an era where the gains of steady economic growth were shared across income groups, helped by a redistributive tax system (Riddell, 2003). Income gaps were consequently narrowing. Levels of poverty fluctuated, but were to decline a decade later (Stewart *et al*, 2009).

The balance of wealth started to change from the 1980s. Unemployment now rose sharply (peaking at 11% in 1993), and the percentage of workless households doubled to 16 per cent by 1997, with the number of children in them the highest in the industrialised world. Earnings disparities grew: the top 10 per cent of male earners saw their remuneration rise by 40 per cent during this period, while those for the bottom 10 per cent stagnated. In 1979, the net incomes of the top tenth of earners were about five times those of the bottom tenth; by the mid-nineties, this figure had roughly doubled (*ibid*:2). Between 1979 and 1997, the proportion of children living in relative poverty had doubled from one in eight to one in four. Pensioner poverty stood at 21 per cent. The social class gradient steepened for life expectancy and child mortality (*ibid*).

After the Labour Government was elected in 1997 there was some progress. Overall, while faster income growth remained among top earners, there was no significant change in the incomes ratio between the top and the bottom 10 per cent. 'Across the distribution, incomes (became) more equally distributed' over a ten year period' (Sefton *et al*, 2009:25). The previous rapid divergence in incomes had halted, albeit with the overall gap remaining. That was not quite true for the top 1 per cent or 0.1 per cent, however: the median earnings of the top FTSE 100 Chief Executives grew by more than 100 per cent between 1999 and 2006, while those for all full time employees only grew about 10 per cent (Sefton *et al*, 2009). Before housing costs, the percentage of children living in poverty declined by 4.4 per cent between 1996/7 and 2006/7, and that of pensioners by 1.4 per cent, but after housing costs, the figure for pensioners goes up to 10.2 per cent. Nevertheless, both figures worsened between 2005 and 2007 (Brewer *et al*, 2008).

These differences remained stubborn, despite the implementation of a range of measures: a national minimum wage, various tax credit schemes, income support for older people, winter fuel payments and so on. And what lay behind these income differences were the social differences which lead to not only the differences in life expectancy and child mortality but also the continuing attainment gaps between children in schools serving different communities, and between those entitled to free school meals and those who are not (Power *et al*, 2002; Sutton Trust, 2009b).

All these matters receive attention from Governments from time to time, but much more intractable than inequalities in circumstance are inequalities in opportunity. Despite there having been universal secondary education for sixty years and the development of mass higher education in the last twenty, generally advantage carries on into the next generation, disadvantage in all its relative forms remains, and what success young people from less advantaged backgrounds achieve at school is not translated straightforwardly into radically different social trajectories from those of their families.

In fact, UK society is underpinned by a social structure of institutions which works to ensure generational succession. This book provides snapshots of this structure at work: how institutions such as independent schools and prestigious universities favour the maintenance of advantage and its passage from one generation to another. And it shows also how the structure of the words we use encourages ideas in some young people about particular social, educational and occupational trajectories – imagined futures – but makes them difficult to conceive by others. Further, the words we use to denote achievement – such as gifted, or talented, or intelligent, or bright – subliminally denote personal worth, so that those young people who do not achieve highly in school or afterwards believe they deserve failure and all that follows from it, rather like my elderly lady apologising for the hole in her wall. Word structures underpin the institutional structures of our society by framing the way we think about ourselves.

The UK is naturally resistant to change. Whereas NGOs such as Amnesty International may enlist celebrities such as Bono, Bob Geldorf or Angelina Jolie to speak out about injustice and what should be done about it, the politicians who wield power in the UK rarely do so. And the current state of affairs, with minor adjustments only, is often assumed to be *totally natural* not only by politicians, but also by those who run the media, large corporations and institutions like universities. The popular belief is that talent can (and does) find its own true way.

It is possible to speculate on the reasons for politicians' reluctance to combat injustice openly in our society – the purported reliance on powerful interests such as financial institutions, for example, or timidity in the face of offending what they see as their supporting interests, a lack of confidence in taking them on. But the reality is that another aspect of social structure is the non-emergence to positions of power, through our party political structures and our major institutions, of the people who would seriously challenge the status quo, despite many words expended on creating the opposite impression. And the nature of the policies they develop, old and new, confirms this.

Background to the book

The work for this book began with my bidding successfully for a small British Academy grant that was awarded in 2005.

My previous work (for example, Riddell, 2003, 2007) had examined what was going on in and around urban schools. Beyond the obvious social disadvantage, I tried to identify what was maintaining the attainment gap, despite the application of school improvement fixes agreed across the English-speaking world. I drew on my professional dilemmas as a local authority officer serving urban areas, including Director of Education in Bristol.

In trying to elucidate such dilemmas, I have tried to take proper account of the effects of social structure, formation, society – whatever you want to call it – which constrain the opportunities available to us and how we might think about them, while seeking out what we can do: the agentic action through which individuals challenge restraints and create social progress.

I draw on some key notions and develop some of my own. Particularly in this book, I draw on Bourdieu's notion of *habitus*, the 'embodied dispositions' we all carry, formed by previous social experience of all kinds (see Bourdieu and Passeron, 1977; Bourdieu and Wacquant, 1992). Habitus frames and interprets new encounters and situations, and helps us decide what to do. It is social structure in the head, 'working in and through people's dispositions, rather than on them' (Ball, 2003a: 16).

At the same time, I have been taken over the years with the models developed by Andrew Pollard and various colleagues, who see learning itself as an iterative social process, of encounters in different contexts, with outcomes being determined by the rules which govern in each (Pollard with Filer, 1996; Pollard and Triggs, 2000). Drawing on Pollard's notion of *epistemic identity* I have emphasised the importance of the relationship between learning experiences in school and those which take place in the other contexts of young people's lives: family, peer group in school and outside, and community (physical and virtual).

Such notions allow us to understand how what I identify as *learning disadvantage* arises when the assumptions and cultural constitution of the classroom are at odds with those in the rest of children's lives – the case in many urban schools – and to develop advice about bridging social experience into teaching and learning, that is, what we should be doing about such learning disadvantage. There need to be urban curricula and pedagogies (Riddell, 2003, 2007).

But the learning of each cohort of middle class children continues to race away cyclically and cumulatively over time through these processes, and is reflected in the widening attainment gaps from age seven onwards in the UK. That of working class children does not. So after my last book, which concentrated on schools (*Schools for Our Cities*, 2003), I became interested in the social processes in the families and communities of middle class children which more broadly form their habitus and give them such educational advantage. These include drawing on their families' social capital, the social resources possessed by family, friends and more distant acquaintances in their network. And I began to ask myself whether or not it would be possible to develop equivalent resources to work for working class children.

The research

Hence the research project was originally entitled 'developing social capital for working class students'. In the course of the research, I interviewed parents and staff at two independent schools in different parts of England to gain some insight into the processes at home and school which led to the development of ambition and aspiration. I discussed the drivers behind current national policy to reduce disadvantage with senior officials in the then DfES (now the DCFS), HM Treasury and the Office of the Deputy Prime Minister (now the DCLG). I visited and interviewed national and local staff of programmes such as Aim Higher; that for the Gifted and Talented; services such as Connexions; and national and local charities dealing with the disengaged (and in this case some of their clients). And finally I visited and interviewed academic and administrative staff concerned with admissions at three universities – one of the Oxbridges, one other Russell Group and one new, post-92 university.

This came to over 50 interviews, best understood, I think, as a series of micro-studies which together provide the snapshots of UK social structure at work in the early 2000s. This was a daunting programme for me as a sole researcher, and the people interviewed do not represent either a random or a stratified sample. But these are real snapshots of actual social processes, interpreted by the people experiencing them. So in each Chapter I consider what these snapshots might be telling us more broadly.

Aspirational identity and social structure

I do say things in the book about social capital (Chapter 2), but what most struck me about the interview data from the parents was that they were implementing a managed model of social reproduction: all the social experiences of their children were constrained, maximising the emergence of the right sorts of views about themselves and appropriate ambitions. So the notion of aspirational identity I developed to explain this model became central to my thinking. It is a different facet of identity from the epistemic I mentioned above, but is related to it. And when I applied this notion to the contexts of the lives of either aspirant working class students (Chapters 5 and 6) or the disengaged (Chapter 7), it was obvious how fragile the process could be for the former and how potentially morbid for the latter. This, again, is social structure at work. Most particularly, it became clear that the current format of national and local programmes will not quite hit the spot for these young people.

The UK government has published a number of policy and strategy documents over the years, but after the advent of the Brown government, a new suite of papers began to appear that were directly concerned with social mobility, a theme which will no doubt continue. In the book, I use the data from my research to interpret these various documents and argue that, although social mobility is likely to increase as a result of government policy, in the sense that greater proportions of generations born in the twenty-first century will be able to improve their social circumstances compared to their parents, the wider social transformation, which would result from the top echelons of the civil service, major companies, the armed forces, the professions and politics being genuinely and equally open to people of working class origin, will take longer and require more work.

This would need a much more explicit project that was redistributive of opportunity and candid about its effects on current structures of opportunity (and dis-opportunity). As the Brecht poem says, this would elicit far more than the wisely nodding heads which follow current muted criticisms of social power.

Layout of the book

I present the evidence from the schools in Chapters 2, 3 and 4. Chapter 4, which includes what the parents said about life outside school, I develop the notion of aspirational identity and a framework for understanding its iterative development.

In Chapter 5, I apply the notion and framework to the circumstances of those working class students identified as having the potential to be the first in their families to attend university. I look at whether the various AimHigher and Gifted and Talented programmes will make a difference and consider the relevance of wider government policy interventions. I conclude that they will, but will do so by becoming the new structural routes to social success for an ennobled minority of the working class, in a way analogous to grammar schools in the past. So they will not bring about social transformation. I argue that the notions of ability and identified potential which underpin these programmes are not unproblematic and contribute to ontological insecurity.

In Chapter 6, I examine how the universities described their admissions processes and find that the narrative of 'academic potential', identified as the criterion for the two prestigious universities, is not that different from the ways the parents I interviewed described the characteristics of their children, and that these are similar to entitlement narratives commonly found elsewhere. This makes the focused task of human capital-creating much easier for their independent schools prior to university interview.

In Chapter 7 the data of and about disengaged students is presented. These students, faced with a construction of aspirational identity as 'failed', act out what should be understood as a resistance culture. I examine the work of organisations and services to which they are often referred and consider why there is not a national programme of investment in them.

Finally, in Chapter 8 I summarise the findings of the book, consider the data on social mobility and find much to welcome in recent government documents. Nevertheless, I consider that social changes in elite recruitment may prove more elusive.

A brief note on terminology

Universities are very important social institutions in the UK and always have been, whether educating less than ten per cent of the population before the Second World War, or over 40 per cent now. The era of mass higher education has brought many changes, however, including a stratification of its institutions, similar to that of schools, despite the formal equivalence of the qualifications they award.

In stratified systems, who or what is at the top becomes significant, and sure enough public discussion of universities in the UK is littered with such terms as 'old', 'top', 'prestigious', 'selective' or 'highly selective'. Universities have grouped themselves into stratified organisations – the 'Russell Group', the '1994 group' and 'million +'. The terms used sometimes overlap: the Sutton Trust talks about 'leading universities' (2005), but this includes thirteen institutions, whereas the Russell Group includes twenty. And some 'top' universities are certainly not 'old' and were Colleges of Arts and Technology not forty years ago.

Nevertheless, there are deep social and structural processes at work, as I outline in Chapter 6, but the distinctions to be made may be fluid. Throughout the book, therefore, I use the term 'prestigious' to cover universities in the upper strata – let's say defined by league tables – to reflect their social significance. I am more specific if the occasion demands it.

2

What the parents said: parenting, children's ambitions and the resources they draw on

If you want good for your child, you have to present them with the possibility of being able to do their homework and being able to have time and effort; and I sit with my children and I do their homework with them, as I'm doing the dinner ... and this is the point you're getting to, isn't it, about how much input we give them...? *Lynne, Merryweather School*

Introduction

The original intention behind talking to parents at two independent schools in different parts of the country had been to gather data about the strategies used by parents outside London. But I was also seeking some colour, some detail, about how such parents brought resources together to bear on the life projects they had constructed for their children (as reported by Ball, 2003a; Power *et al*, 2003 and others), so that a picture might emerge of how to construct the equivalent for working class children and their parents.

In the event, what they said gave me more than I had anticipated: the managed model of social reproduction (that is, how their children reproduce or better the social and economic circumstances of their parents), referred to in the last Chapter. Although not embodying care-free processes for the parents, this model is robust and could not be imitated easily in different educational or social circumstances. The model and its applicability are developed over the next few Chapters.

The parental microstudy was of parents from eleven families at two independent schools. The parents were chosen by the schools concerned on the basis that they were likely to be able and willing to discuss their experiences and their children with me. I then wrote to them to explain that I was interested in the development of their children's ambitions and aspirations. In the event, one parent dropped out after hearing direct from me, but all the others were willing to discuss their relationships with their children in personal, and sometimes intimate, detail. I am really grateful to them. I interviewed them individually.

The parents were largely middle class (both the parent interviewed and the one who was generally absent), in the sense of having 'privileged work and market situations ... (not being) closely supervised at work (and) ... trusted to use initiative and discretion' (Roberts, 2001:145). Two interviewees were fathers, one occupied what Roberts might term an 'intermediate position' (but she had a first degree), and two owned their own businesses. The class position is interesting, but not essential for understanding the managed model of social reproduction being considered here. It is important, however, for the wider significance of these findings.

In this Chapter, the parents describe their style of parenting, how they discuss their children's ambitions, and the sorts of resources they draw on to help them as their children grow up. Although the parents were identified by the schools, they had children at various stages of their education and not surprisingly discussed children who were at other schools, included state ones. The children of one parent had left both Merryweather School and university and he felt able to reflect over a longer process of his children's formation.

The two schools, Carter's in the south west of England, and Merryweather in the north, are described in the next Chapter.

Generic ambition and 'life projects'
The reflections of the parents I interviewed, and their descriptions of the strategies they used for their children, echoed what Ball (2003a) found and thought about from much bigger data sets elsewhere. In itself this lends support to broader notions of social structure (and habitus) – why should they be thinking the same sorts of things – as

these parents were in two cities in very different parts of the country from Ball's interviewees.

The parents I interviewed were not actively constructing specific life projects, in the sense of named trajectories, but they were interested in a more generic ambition. And they certainly wanted their children to 'come to see the relationships between school, higher education and work as a process', as Ball says (*ibid*:84), and for their children to develop aspirations accordingly. With one exception, the mothers I interviewed were clearly the 'status maintainers' (p144), in the sense of trying to ensure their children got on.

So none of the parents really had a specific career in mind for their children, and this seemed to be a common characteristic. For example:

> ...as a parent my aspirations for my children are for them to have a good general education, for them to take command of their own lives and to do what they really want to do in order to become healthy independent members of society ... So I wouldn't say I wanted my son to be a doctor, (or) I want my daughter to be this, that or the other ... and I think my husband is the same. *Deborah, Carter's*

> ... I don't have any specific things that I want my children to do... *Kate, Carter's*

> ...but ambition-wise, we encourage them to be whatever they want to be. At this point in time...they haven't got a specific (career in mind) *Lynne, Merryweather*

> ... so yeah, we don't say too much. I have to say they really have to make their own choices – you don't want to influence them. *Fay, Merryweather*

This thinking is exemplified in the following exchange:

> Interviewer: Have you had those sorts of discussions (about specific careers)?

> Jenny, Carter's: No, I wouldn't. I don't know, because I don't actually have anything in my mind that I want them to be.

> Interviewer: No?

> Jenny: So I can't say I've ever said to them: 'Oh, I want you to do whatever'. I just have a sense that for instance, they do this sort of aptitude sort of thing, and that's quite good and there are lots of discussion points in that, and that was fine. Obviously with H (my elder daughter), she was very definite in what she wanted....

Jenny's elder daughter was at medical school at the time of the interview.

Interestingly, a number of the interviewees also criticised fellow parents who had very specific trajectories in mind for their children. They were considered excessively 'pushy' and 'controlling' – naked ambition was seen as distasteful. But these comments were also reflexive – were they were doing enough -particularly one parent who described her eldest son at one point as having 'lost his way'. Here are some of these comments:

> I mean, we're not parents who drive them and coach them and give them extra Maths to get in or anything. We've always rather despised that – sort of negative snobbery – and said, 'well, if they're not up to it that's fine'. But we do want to give them the opportunities that they are up to... *Peter, Merryweather*

> I remember having discussions with other mothers about it when J was young ... You know: 'I think your son looks like he's going to be an accountant' ... 'I can see my son as ...'. You know. And I thought that was very bizarre... these tiny children and they were already planning out what they thought they could see them being ... (and) obviously had ideas about good jobs and what they wanted their sons to be. And I just wanted him to have the opportunities, I wanted him to be happy, and I wanted him to have a choice ... *Kerry, Merryweather*

> M has friends who have parents who say you are going to be a doctor and I find that unbelievable. I don't know how you can ... *Charlotte, Merryweather*

The following exchange also illustrates this sort of thinking among the parents:

> Ann, Carter's: I mean I'm afraid I have probably done a lot of influencing, I mean when I talk about my job...

> Interviewer: Why are you afraid about it?

> Ann: Well... I don't know ... I think I see too many parents who are very pushy with their children, who try to live their own ambitions through their children. You see that particularly on the sports field. I mean at cricket where S plays, one chappie... (pause) his son is very, very talented. And it's quite clear that he's living out his ambitions through his son, he's pushing his son, he's going to be a professional cricketer whether he likes it or not. Now I can't help but think it's sad, I think, parents trying to live out their own ambitions through their children. You know I don't believe you should do that.

These comments were echoed by staff at both the schools, including the Deputy Head at Merryweather, who had been 'accosted' that morning, as he put it, by a parent who wanted her son to be a doctor, and did not think the current quality of chemistry teaching he was receiving was good enough to help her son achieve the right grade (ie an A). So clearly the pursuit of particular career paths was going on (see Chapter 3) if not in this sample.

Nevertheless, and most important, even though the ambition may not be specific, often a generic *type of appropriate* trajectory was assumed. Most commonly, this included university (as in Reay *et al*, 2005), either as a specific aspiration or as part of discussions about careers requiring graduate status. This generic ambition appeared time after time and, again, appears to be a common way of thinking, as in this exchange:

> Kerry, Merryweather: I think education has been the main thing: that's been my priority, to get him a good education and good opportunities. I do hope he'll go to university. I think that would be a brilliant experience and the right thing for him to do. Beyond that...
>
> Interviewer: So it's assumed he's going to university, is it?
>
> Kerry: Yes, I hope so, yes, he's an academic child, he enjoys studying and hopefully we'll find a way of getting him into university... he's always been interested in history and classics right from the start – it's always been his favourite subject.

And later in the same interview, Kerry, a lawyer herself, said the following as part of a longer discussion about having ambitions for their children:

> I don't know, I don't have a particular yen for them to go into law but I would want them to do something professional ... You know you can't help it; I want them to be graduates minimum, and I'd want them to do something professional. At the moment I'd want them to be child and adolescent psychologists, because you don't pay them under ten thousand a report at the moment ... so that would be quite nice and that's the sort of thing A could do, he'd be very good at that. But that sort of thing, you know, something that they ... but also... I want them to enjoy it .... It's always a joke in my house: they've got to be brain surgeons, no pressure! And they laugh at me ... *Kerry, Carter's*

And Ann was also clear:

> I think ... John really feels they should go to university and whilst I agree I think they should, because I think in this day and age it's the norm ... if you don't go you're at a disadvantage because most people will go ... *Ann, Carter's*

This generic ambition among parents has been found elsewhere (see West and Noden, 2003, for example). And the expectation of the two schools was also that not attending university would be exceptional (see Chapter 3).

Proactive parenting: 'presenting possibilities'

All the parents were more or less active in encouraging their children. Even if the actual choice of career was left to them, if there were signs of indecision or uncertainty, or a difficulty in taking a decision forward, the family would get involved. There would sometimes be extensive discussions, trying to encourage an appropriate trajectory and ensure the young person did the right thing. It would be hoped and expected that the trajectory, or appropriate aspiration, would then emerge or re-emerge from the process.

'Proactive' seems an appropriate description of the common style of parenting in this group. It goes beyond a passive interest and dutiful attendance at formal events to hear about the performance of their children. It involves taking the initiative, seizing opportunities, questioning what they are told, and trying to ensure their children worked sufficiently hard, got the most out of school and made the appropriate moves and choices. Here are some examples:

> Deborah, Carter's: I just pestered them continuously, but again ... I never ever had to remind S to do revision, prepare homework or anything, but S and J... I was always on J's back because he would always much rather do other things. S less so than J, but when it comes to stuff she enjoys like English and theatre studies, she's self-motivated. I was very aware of the weaker teachers, and so on occasions have had to put a little bit of input in there and to help kids to survive a particular teacher.
>
> Interviewer: So you've coached them through it?
>
> Deborah: I've coached them through it, yeah.

Another parent talked about her son who had just started thinking about a particular career in the services:

Interviewer: Have you talked to J about his ambitions? I mean before he started thinking about going into the army?

Jenny, Carter's: We've talked to him about all sorts of things, but I think initially he wanted to be a professional sportsman. I think that would have been his (first choice)... but I think as time goes on you realise how tenuous (sport) all is.

Jenny contrasts her son with her daughter, who was always clear what she wanted to do (and was doing it at the time of the interview), but whom she still coached extensively through the process of thinking about university:

Interviewer: You took her there, did you?

Jenny: Oh yeah, we went and we did the thing, and we did the sheet and the fors and the againsts, and we looked at the security, and how far you'd have to walk, and how far your money would go and all those sorts of things to make the decision. J is not so easy, because I say: 'which are we going to look at?' And he sort of just mumbles... So I've given him, in my mind ... I was talking about it last night actually ... I've given him until his last AS and then I'm on his case in a sort of nice way.

But she had also been active in helping her son J consider a career in the services:

....we did speak to someone in the DG Regiment because they're disbanding. So I got some information on that, picked up various bits and pieces and ploughed through it.

Another parent at the same school, Ann, gave numerous examples about the sorts of reflexive processes they were going through: should they intervene? Should they be more relaxed in the pressure they were creating?

...with T doing his GCSEs I used to harangue him about the fact he wasn't doing revision ... Whereas this time round ... OK, I make comments: 'have you done your revision' ... but I haven't really ... I've been much more relaxed about it and I've got to the stage where I'm thinking 'he's got to work it out for himself ... but he's got to do it if he wants to get the grades he wants'. Whereas with my daughter I don't have the same problem at all, in that she's very organised, she knows what she's got to do and I wouldn't dream of interfering ... a very different attitude.

But the following comment shows that she hasn't been all that relaxed about it:

> ...actually pinning him down and actually getting him to learn is very challenging, but part of it is a little innate arrogance that they don't think that they need to do it.

And Ann describes clearly the proactive but reflexive role in constructing an appropriate trajectory:

> ... (from) the sort of discussions we've had I think he probably is thinking that he will end up being an accountant or something like that ... So one of the things that we did research together, we had a look at accountancy: you either could do your accountancy exam ... but actually they were more interested in ... well as far as they were concerned as long as you had a degree, it didn't matter what it was in....

And again, this time with an explicit endorsement from her son for her role:

> We went together to an open day at... Uni, and we went to the accountancy thing and ... I think we both agreed that accountancy was not really the thing to do and, so ... I was quite surprised, but he's ... wanted a parent with him at these open days, so we've gone together...

Peter, at Merryweather, described a process of whole family involvement around significant 'milestones, which were sometimes difficult':

> ... and in those cases of big family decisions we've always sat down around the kitchen table. We're a kitchen table family. We got a big piece of paper and wrote down the pros and cons of every school, whether it was transport or education possibilities or the ethos of the school and so on. In their words, they mapped it out very clearly...

Another father, Adrian, did not give such examples from his two (now adult) sons' time in school, but the following comment shows that active intervention does not cease upon entrance to university:

> And an example was when I badgered R to queue for his apartment in London: he was really whinging about it because he didn't want to commit himself, that's the thing. When he was first in the queue, he rang up and said, 'sorry I doubted you', you know. *Adrian, Merryweather*

Lynne's comments on 'presenting possibilities' headed up this Chapter. This mother of two boys, one at Merryweather, one in the state sector, explained how she thought about the process. Charlotte, also with a son at Merryweather and a daughter formerly in the state sector, illustrated the sorts of discussions and activities which had gone on in her household. First with respect to her son:

> We were discussing it last night. He thinks he's a rung below Oxbridge. He's got friends who are applying to Oxbridge who've done better at examinations. But he, I don't know, I just think he didn't want to go there. Because his dad went, I don't know.

And her daughter:

> (I) just kept on giving her ideas as to what she would like to do and she latched onto physiotherapy. I can't say that she particularly wanted to do that but that's what she is doing, she is in her second year now. ... So we sort of bullied her into looking around universities and we took her around the country and um, (pause) yeah. I took her for a careers evening ... yes I think we had a careers evening.

And finally, another mother discusses what she needs to do for a seemingly retiring son:

> He knows what he wants to do, but he is very reluctant to push himself forward ever, so you have to push him in the right direction. He'll do it: ... he knows what he has to do, but he's reluctant to do it. I do intervene – you have to. He is better than he was, but he's still quiet. *Fay, Merryweather*

Parents in other social circumstances are also proactive, but in working class families, this may be more focused in ensuring they are happy and safe and not in trouble at school, and less on future educational, occupational and social trajectories (Gillies, 2007).

Resources outside the family

The data so far, demonstrating the reflexive strategising used by these parents, are consonant with previous findings (eg Lareau, 2000; Ball 2003a; Vincent and Ball, 2006). Similarly, we know that middle class parents draw on their social capital to help them navigate their children's trajectories, particularly at key decision making points (Power *et al*, 2003a). Social capital, in the sense of Putnam (2000) or Halpern (2005), here means information, advice or preferment available from members of their families', schools' and others' contacts, their so-called 'weak ties' (Granovetter, 1973). And there were many examples of using social capital in this way in these interviews. The point that:

> (The) young people are able to mobilise relationships and obligations which parents, other relatives and friends are part of or can access... (Ball, 2003a: 84)

was illustrated time after time.

Here are some of the many examples of the availability and use of such social capital in helping to form aspiration and negotiate barriers. First, Jenny describes the process whereby her daughter first began to decide she wanted to be a doctor:

> ...Being in Farthering (village school), she was friends with a lot of people whose parents were doctors... (The headteacher) used to say 'I think the wind blows across from Farthering (hospital) and infects them', and she used to laugh... She had a little friend and they were from Iceland ... he was a plastic surgeon and she was quite interested in that. And then she had another friend and he was the thing at the burns unit, and she would ask him all sorts of things, and Andrew (my husband) would say: 'gosh, she's very interested. I don't know whether I should be discussing these things with her, she's quite young'... *Jenny, Carter's*

And again, describing how they got their son through the difficulty of being dropped by one of the local professional football clubs:

> When he was fourteen ... he was dropped from the (professional football club). He ... had been with them since he was nine. He thought his world had fallen apart ... And I think if he'd not had school and mixing with his best friend ... whose father ... was the (County Cricket) coach ... (W)hen it happened, we rang J to tell him ... (He) has a very great interest and some professional qualifications in sports psychology ... and so we went round there and J spent a lot of time with him working it all through and talking about it.

Jenny also went on to describe the rest of her network(s):

> And also we're part of Christchurch ... and we have huge amounts of people ... we have loads of people we can talk to, professionals in their own right ... I mean Deborah's husband is (a) Professor, and one of his colleagues at ... he's the head of psychology and whatever ... there's always somebody you can get hold of.

Kate describes how she had used a friend to make contact with a tutor when her son was having difficulties with literacy, and another who gave her encouragement. This quote also shows her own anxiety for her children:

> ... and she's a special needs teacher and she put me on to a friend of hers who sees children. So once a week for a term A used to go to this lady just to help him understand verbal reasoning ... and because she was so good and so lovely, (my other son) goes to her for a little extra help for his English. And we're going to stop that now at the end of the year because we think he's coming on ...
>
> ... but then I've got this (other) friend ... She's ... a barrister ... an incredible intellect, (and) she knows my children really well and she always says to me (my children are fine) ... but you know her children, I'm thinking, are doing better ... *Kate, Carter's*

Peter at Merryweather describes in the following exchange the advice they sought when their son was having difficulties:

> Peter: Some of the things we've mentioned with H, for instance, are of huge concern to us, so we've talked widely to anyone we can find ... It is a network of people we know, from the parish, friends and family. So we've gone to the head of special learning and that sort of thing. In terms of careers and opportunities ... we're very privileged in a way ... we've got a big network of people we can draw on, from our own parents downwards. We've always done that.
>
> Interviewer: Have you had to do that much?
>
> Peter: Not at all. We've done it a little bit with (our other son), thinking about what he might do for his career ... One of his Godparents is a stockbroker, so... We've also got contacts in the RAF – we got (another of our sons) gliding.

Charlotte described the importance of the network acquired by her husband's being chair of governors at their local primary school (several parents mentioned partners or close relatives being involved as governors in the state sector):

> (My daughter's university) were very keen that she had lots of work experience, so we were having to ring friends ... We have got friends who can be called on for favours really, so she got her work experience from friends and contacts, because my husband was a parent-governor at primary school. So he got to know a few parents and ... so we drew on that. *Charlotte, Merryweather*

Fay describes her efforts to help her son at Merryweather apply successfully to Cambridge, drawing on her social capital. He wanted to be a vet. This was an interesting discussion, because this parent did not feel she was getting all the advice she needed from the school. The event is one of the clearest examples from the interviews of the mobilisation of social capital:

> ... of course we use networks that we know and we don't know any vets. But we do know people that have got children into veterinary school, so we've asked them for their experience. And we've got friends that ... we've got a friend who is Professor of Dentistry at (this University). He's looked at the (Universities and Colleges Admissions Service) form, he's looked at the personal statement, things like that; so we have used contacts, for sure, to make sure that we're doing it properly. We got the book on how to get in to veterinary science ...

> ... and my parents both went to Cambridge, and my godparents. My godfather is Professor ... at Cambridge. So for instance last night ... they came back with this Cambridge form and the teacher said 'if you haven't got anything positive to say on the square ... don't put anything in it'. So I thought 'that's a bit odd, if they don't put anything ... It doesn't look very keen if you don't put anything else', so I rang up my godfather and said 'what do you think here, should we put something in this space? And if so, what should I put?'

> So I do, you know, (use contacts). And then his teacher here said 'don't apply to Y (College) because um, that's really difficult to get into, it's very popular, go for one of the rubbish ones' or something. He said to (my son) 'go for one of the rubbish colleges'. So I said 'what does he think one of the rubbish colleges at Cambridge is?'. So that didn't make sense to me.

> Well, I said to my godfather 'what have you got to say on this as well? You know, is St. John's too ambitious, should we try somewhere else, does it make any difference, I thought there was a pool system blah, blah'. And he said 'no, just tell him to apply for St John's; if they want him at Cambridge they will offer ... or put him in the pool. Do that'.

And with respect to her daughter, at a nearby girls' independent school, who has expressed an interest in being a human rights lawyer, Fay says:

> ... and she has just developed her interest from really enjoying (Religious Studies). She has got a superb teacher there who I have to say really nurtures it, brings in a lot of cuttings from newspapers, lots of good discussion and ... that's where she's got her interest from. We have got friends that are lawyers, and so we will be contacting them, if that's what she wants to do, who will be happy to put her in touch with people for work experience.

And finally for Fay, she was able to take advice when her son was having difficulty earlier on in his school career, at another school, which involved conflict with a teacher:

> ... we had legal (advice) ... one of our friends is a lawyer who helped us with that side of things, but it was a protracted battle.

Geraldine, also with a son at Merryweather, and a daughter at the same girls' independent school, described the development of her daughter's ambition to be an architect:

> Geraldine: ... (our daughter) was looking at architecture, then she had some work experience, with architects, which she liked ... And I think that gave her a bit of an insight into internal structures and the uses of materials in buildings, and I think that's where it might have come from ... She did two weeks with somebody and, you know, it was very good.
>
> Interviewer: Was that a placement she found herself?
>
> Geraldine: Yes, somebody we knew. And it was interesting because he said 'yes, but it's two weeks'. He said 'I don't think it is worth doing anything less than two weeks'.

But she had also considered other placements for her other daughter:

> We did discuss work experience ... with a friend who works for Rothschild's ... for my daughter, but they only do university-type ones anyway.

And similarly to Fay, Geraldine had also had a detailed discussion about admission to Cambridge, drawing on 'weak ties' (see above):

> Geraldine: Interesting thing was that when we had an informal chat with somebody last year, who was a fellow at (Cambridge College), he said there's two interviews. One is the sort of technical, scientific, subject one. And he said at St. John's the other one is more the pastoral one – you know: about you and whatever, that sort of thing. But my daughter applied to (another College) ...
>
> Interviewer: This fellow at Cambridge: was he a friend or contact?
>
> Geraldine: Uh, he was a sort of friend, not someone we knew terribly well ... he used to work for my husband's previous company, not when my husband was there, but we met him socially. But somebody e-mailed him and he was very happy to see us, so we just went in the summer and had a look, and had a chat with him. We took another friend ... In the end he's gone to Oxford, he didn't like Cambridge.

And finally, Geraldine describes the principal context for the social capital they draw on, and a major potential influence on her children:

> I mean we have a very good group of friends, with a range of ... children, whatever. You know – all just a year apart ... and we sort of, we have a lot of discussions with them about all sorts of different things ... And we sort of pick up bits from them, or we pick up people to talk to about certain things, you know. And that works very well: people we see quite regularly, through the sports club. And the children they all get on, they are not the best of friends, but they all get on fine...
>
> ... and there's a mixture of ... backgrounds. One of our friends is a GP ... Again somebody else is in a similar business to my husband but is ex-Cambridge, you know; one or two teachers; and we all talk about unis as well, and different things. One or two have got older ones who are at university and talk about the courses there and things, so we just have to do that.

The validity of these data

A common picture of proactive parenting emerges from these two groups of parents. They shared many common assumptions about what is right for their children and what they should pursue. Despite the proactivity, they were not unthinking and clearly did not assume they had done the right things in the past or would do in the future. Nearly all of them had relatives, friends or contacts whom they called on in one way or another to further their children's educational, occupational, and hence, social, trajectories.

The interviews may have privileged some of this data. The parents may have overstated their proactivity, as they knew the subject of the interview in advance, and might have consciously or unconsciously wished to present a positive view of their parenting, perhaps exaggerating their efforts. The interview itself provided an opportunity for reflection, which they may not have taken before.

Did the parents exaggerate? Maybe so in discussions of some matters, but there was no question of the authenticity of their discussion and reflections, illustrated from experience. Staff in the schools described cases of proactivity among their parents, such as the mother of the aspirant medic mentioned earlier. In some circumstances, this is precisely what schools describe as parents being difficult, and in turn some of these parents were by no means uncritical of their children's schools.

But the similarity between the descriptions of approaches they had taken in particular circumstances – across two schools 150 miles apart – was striking. Moreover, the discourse of these parents echoes that found in the other studies cited above; this is what reinforces the notion of social structure discussed in Chapter 1.

What these parents represent

The degree of proactivity will of course vary among these parents and over time. We do know though that middle class parents are proactive in many contexts, as these are, and in England, they are so even in the apparently most unpromising contexts for them (James and Beedell, 2009; more on this study later in the book). But the managed model of social reproduction (and the formation of aspiration) which I develop over the next few Chapters does not depend on the proactivity of parents; the proactivity determines how well it works for *individual children*. As I argue, the act of choice itself in selecting independent schools presents parents with a framework for managing social reproduction which is likely to be more reliable than that available in other contexts.

But these parents – and thousands of others – also bring significant resources to this reliable framework for social reproduction. Consider carefully the examples of social capital given in the interviews. If you know someone at Rothschild's, have a godparent who is a Cambridge professor, have a General Practitioner in your friendship group, or have acquaintances who are architects, it is because of who, and most importantly, what you are and in what social circles you move. These social capitals, and the other capitals these children can access, are there because you occupy a certain position in the social structure.

Social capital, in this sense, is not merely *neutral* networks in the ways described above, or perhaps by Putnam and Halpern. As Bourdieu makes clear (1986), it is *inscribed* in, is a result of, and is in itself part of, social structure. Such capital is therefore natural for the parents interviewed. Unskilled and skilled members of the working class are unlikely to have people occupying such social and professional positions in their personal networks, without intervention, and it begins to be clear that such intervention would need to be a major undertaking.

3

The schools' view of things

...the process is underway and they should be thinking about it ... it's a kind
of drip feed that just builds and builds. *Head of Sixth, Merryweather School*

Introduction

My interviews with senior staff at the two schools focused on the
motivation of children, raising aspirations, the role models
drawn on (and in) by the schools, the role of the tutor, and communications with parents.

One of the striking things to come out of the school visits was how
much the staff's views (and school publications and websites) mirrored
the expectations voiced by parents, particularly of a trajectory for young
people that included university. In addition, whole aspects of school
life, and the internal processes described by staff, by which pupils were
expected to develop and achieve the right aspirations, graphically illustrated the sort of 'institutional habitus' described in such schools by
Reay *et al* (2005). By that, they meant the concerted combination of
processes, expressed and expected values, and rewarded behaviours in
school, which help condition the expectations and pathways of students and, most importantly, their decision making.

As a lifelong advocate of comprehensive education, both as a teacher
and an LA officer, I was very impressed by both schools. Among other
things, I found the openness of staff commendable, given they may well
have expected I was coming to criticise them. I admired the huge
academic subject enthusiasm of the teachers I met, which made me

think more than once that I would have liked to have been taught by them. And perhaps most impressive of all, I was struck by the confidence, courtesy and respect shown by the pupils, including in one case to a most tedious outside speaker in an upper school assembly, where there were no little signs of inattention rippling through the audience.

This is no doubt a statement about my own middle class professional social values. But, when you consider what the schools are able to do, and many, if not most, state schools are not in a position to, the relationship between independent schools and prestigious universities begins to be seen for what it is: a key part of our social structure.

The schools
Before looking at what the staff said, I briefly introduce the two schools. I am basing this on the schools' own publications and websites, reports from the Independent Schools Inspection Service and my own observations on visit.

Carter's School, in the southwest, was founded in the eighteenth century by a philanthropist as a school for poor boys. It has been coeducational since the 1990s, and at the time of writing had a 'lower school' with just over 200 pupils to year 6, and an 'upper school' of 600 pupils, including 160 in the sixth form. Just over 5 per cent of the pupils in the upper school were boarders.

The school describes itself on its website as one of the region's 'leading independent schools'. The school is selective, with 'assessments' being generally available for entry at 7+, 9+ and 11+. However, pupils also enter the school after assessment at 13+ (as in public schools, after the common entrance exam), and 16, for sixth form education, for which entry is by interview and on the basis of GCSE results. Like many independent schools, Carter's offers scholarships and bursaries.

Besides its academic record, the school boasts of the quality of its pastoral care and programmes for PSE. It says that it admits 'a broad mix of pupils from different social backgrounds', which, it believes, 'naturally encourages tolerance, understanding and an appreciation of others' (school website). It was not possible to verify all these claims during the days of interviewing, but the most recent inspection report describes the 'excellent pastoral care' and 'the very high level of personal development of each pupil'. The parents interviewed echoed these views, with some referring to it as 'comprehensive' in its intake, including children with special needs. Several mentioned the positive atmosphere at the school that had been a reason for choosing the school in the first place and had helped make their children confident once there.

The school has been accommodated on a former ecclesiastical site for over 100 years and occupies older ivy-grown buildings and more modern ones. It is known locally for the quality of its sports provision, and on visiting the school at any time of the year, you will come across students on their way to and from organised games.

Merryweather School in the north of England is a different kettle of fish. It is in the tradition of northern boys' grammar schools, originally being founded in the sixteenth century. Like many, it had a spell as a direct grant school following the 1944 education act (whereby the vast majority of its costs were state-funded), but reverted to full independent status in the mid-1970s. It is highly selective, with entrance examinations being held early each year, and highly academic. It advertises itself on its website as a school 'for the top 5 per cent of boys in the country', with 'results among the very best in the country', and employing 'top academic staff'. The latest inspection report, again, seems to endorse these claims: the text is sprinkled with many 'outstandings'.

At the time of my visits, there were about 1300 boys on roll, with some 400 of them in the sixth form. About 200 boys in the school were in receipt of bursary support, with the rest being fee-paying. Roughly half the intake, the school says, comes from non-fee-paying maintained schools, but the school recently opened its own junior department for years 5 and 6. The school occupies a large site in a residential area, where it moved between the wars. The following self-description of the school signifies how it sees its work of preparing its pupils for later life:

> We encourage our pupils to recognise that admissions tutors (and, later, employers) look for people who are self-confident, and who can think quickly and independently. *Merryweather Prospectus*

What the staff said

Expectations and institutional habitus

In some contrast to the consistent theme of raising aspirations in UK government policy for the past ten years – from the launch of the Excellence in Cities scheme (DfEE, 1999) to the 2009 social mobility white paper (Cabinet Office, 2009a) – staff at the two schools did not report themselves as doing much work which might be construed as aspirational or motivational. What they did describe, however, was an *unspoken assumption* of achievement, including expectation of progression to university, running as a thread through all the contexts of school life, particularly as the students got older. It is this which is fundamental to the institutional habitus.

The following quote is a good illustration of this assumption of the everyday *normality* of what they do. I put it to the head of sixth form at Merryweather that the school was adept at coaching and preparing for Oxbridge and other prestigious universities (which is what the parents said they wanted):

> We do have Oxbridge lessons, in (the first year 6th Form), which is just stretching their Chemistry or History or something like that – just getting them to think a bit more beyond the syllabus. There's a course which gets them to speed up their ability to do questions that might be on the test, like the one all medics do now. I wouldn't say it's coaching, it's just further education.

The assumption of normality for this sort of work is redolent of the famous remark of Bourdieu about the fish in water:

> ... And when habitus encounters a social world of which it is a product, it is like a 'fish in water': it does not feel the weight of the water, and it takes the world about itself for granted. (Bourdieu and Wacquant, 1992:127)

In other words, students come from a home background with the sorts of habitus-forming expectations we have seen in the previous Chapter. They then enter the school environment, where these expectations are echoed, and immediately feel at home. And then they encounter them again when they are called for an interview at a prestigious university, for which they have been prepared, as we shall see.

30

What the schools do

The drip feed process

So, what are the practices which engender and maintain such an institutional habitus? Although there were differences in emphasis between the two schools, staff mentioned broadly the same things:

- a relentless focus in school events on achievement in various fields;

- an emphasis by all staff on academic work and preparation for university;

- the positive influence on students exercised by individual members of staff, particularly their *choices of subject* at university (very often influence meant emulation in this sense);

- the links maintained by staff, and particularly heads of department, with prestigious universities;

- the central role of the head of sixth form in guiding staff and students through the various stages of supported choosing, applying for and being accepted by university, with the steps laid out in detail;

- the related and coordinating role of sixth form tutors;

- programmes of invited outside speakers – including alumni – emphasising very often professional goals, and giving out information about how 'people like you' can achieve them (ie former students at this school, with whom current ones could identify);

- careers and university conferences, emphasising the higher education route.

Some of these practices are found in state schools, of course, and these particular features, particularly post-16, are very similar to those found by Sutton Trust-commissioned research into state schools reputed, in their terms, to be 'good at' getting poorer students into 'top' universities (Curtis *et al*, 2008). These schools had been hard to identify at first, but in them too, the goal of university entrance was almost the only focus post-16, despite the original intake. These features will of course also be found in state 11-18 schools, and possibly sixth form colleges, serving more affluent areas with a large throughput to higher education. In other areas, we know both from this Sutton Trust study and Raphael Reed *et al* (2007), that they are not found.

But in these two independent schools – reflecting the parental aspirations described in the last Chapter – the almost exclusive assumption and focus on progress to higher education, including pre-16, is critical to understanding the institutional habitus of the whole school. State schools generally everywhere have to take into account a wider range of aspirations and destinations.

The following comments exemplify the institutional habitus:

> We don't have many parents who don't ... I can't think of many at all that wouldn't want their children to go to university and want them instead to go directly to employment because that's what the family needs. *Head, Carter's*

> ... but you just don't come across anybody who's thinking 'education is not for me', or 'education plus training is not for me'. They don't think like that. They see this place as stepping stone onto university, professional training and a career of some sort ... without necessarily having any idea of what that career will be. *Deputy Head, Merryweather*

> Every time I put a notice in assembly, it's on the basis of assuming they are all university applicants. *Head of Sixth, Merryweather*

The head of sixth at Merryweather went on to describe clearly and eloquently how the process of getting into university is broken down into manageable steps. An extract from this longer comment from the head of sixth heads this Chapter.

> ... and then what happens is, at the start of sixth form, we actually start saying, 'well, you've got to start thinking about what you want to do when you leave here, because although you've just entered the sixth form, the process of applying to university will start next March. And next March you will go to a careers convention at (the) ... University where you will see lots of things from other universities and you'll think Bristol looks nice, or whatever ... and then between then and Easter we will have various talks with you about how the UCAS process works: you'll have a form to fill in, and then as soon as you come back after Easter, we will start the interviewing process ... which is one by one, going through, starting with those people who know what they want to do and are probably going to get the grades ... We'll talk to you about what you want to do and we will then, on the basis of that interview and your teachers' comments, we will start to write your draft UCAS reference, ready

to be sent off in September.' So all the way through (the lower sixth), they're being told the process is underway and they should be thinking about it... it's a kind of drip feed that just builds and builds ... and we say 'if you're thinking about doing medicine, or vet science, or dentistry, then get some work experience', you know, because if you haven't got the work experience it might be too late ... Some of these things you can't leave until you apply. In addition to that, we have a careers conference run by (the head of careers) in November ...

But both schools start the careers advice earlier than that, because of the importance of the appropriate choice of A Levels for particular careers:

They make that choice in the fourth year, and at that point we give them some careers advice. We say 'if there is any possibility that you may want to do Medicine, for goodness' sake don't drop any sciences at this point because you'll end up taking longer if you haven't got Physics at GCSE', or something like that. So we give them some advice at that stage about what they shouldn't drop, just to keep the doors open. In (Year 11), we say to them, 'if you really know what you want to do as a career – if you want to be a vet, for instance – then there are certain things you have to do. But for most of you, you don't know yet what you want to do, so the best thing to do is choose subjects that you are enjoying at the moment and that you're good at'. And it's the same all the way through the school. *Head of Sixth, Merryweather*

...all through they have to apply for things. The whole focus on potential careers and aspirations is really developed from year nine onwards. *Head, Carter's*

The 'drip feed that just builds and builds' referred to by the head of sixth at Merryweather, with the rigorous progress towards university, is present at both schools:

... So (the head of post-16) keeps a historic record of what people with those GCSEs got in years gone by, what the highest achievement was and what the lowest achievement was, where you are at the moment, what you're tracking for, and every assessment time they get that fed back to them twice a term. And I would have said in the sixth form the ambitions for university amongst the group are set pretty early – they go to careers fairs, higher education fairs and they get on with their UCAS forms pretty quickly by the deadlines. And the vast majority will go off to university. That will be their choice and the sorts of courses are quite varied ... *Head, Carter's*

Finally, Jenny, a parent at Carter's, reported an aspect of such a drip feed which worked for her daughter:

> ... with H (who wanted to be a doctor), she was very definite in what she wanted, so it was a case of Mr B (the head of post-16), when she came in to the sixth form, saying: 'we know this is what you want to do H. And this is what we're going to do (for you)'.

Outside speakers and old members of the school

Part of the drip feed is the programme of external visitors, giving the important and formative message to current pupils about the achievements of their predecessors. To judge from the interviews, the programme was not quite as developed at Carter's as at Merryweather. Nevertheless, the old pupils' association had managed a scheme using former pupils of the school, and visits from prominent sporting and other personalities were continuing to take place, according to what was said. Many of these visitors were of national standing: Carter's is well-known locally for the importance of its sport in the development of its pupils, for example, as has been mentioned. But there was also a sixth form 'general studies' programme of visiting speakers, with a much wider focus than career and university progression.

The old pupils' association at Carter's was still active in other ways in helping children progress to a chosen career. For example, Jenny, just quoted, also reported that her daughter H '...went on a medilink conference and the (Old Carterians) stumped up some of the money for her to go.'

The following quotations show the extent and use at Merryweather of the developed network of Old Merryweatherians' (OMs). First, Charlotte, who is a parent but also works in the school's development office, which maintains links with OMs:

> ... the old boys and ... this chap Paul A, his picture's on the wall there ... he is an economist and he comes in and talks to the boys. So they have all these old boys ... I know the (Old M's) database, so that if any of the boys at school want any advice about working in London or any of the professions, they can get in touch with them ...There are ... contacts all over the world ...
>
> I organised a reunion a couple of years ago and ... one of them was a doctor, and he just said to me 'if you want a doctor to come, to give a talk about

medicine, you know, what's it like as a career, I'm happy to drive over and give a talk'. So...

And further, a story about an OM who had recently left, and the setting up of 'Doc Soc', related here by the head of careers at Merryweather:

(He had) applied for medicine, a very, very talented young man... He was rejected by Oxford and managed to get himself a place at two other institutions. But basically because of his experience of the whole process of applying for medicine, he decided, after he finished and got his offers and everything, he decided that this wasn't good enough and he wanted to help his peers in the year below, so he started a society which we christened Doc Soc. And he was absolutely inspirational in getting together the group of next year medics and talking to them about his experiences this year. And he brought in lads from his own year group as well – they all shared their experiences ... they met every week and that's continued on this year. ... He made a difference, absolutely no benefit to him whatsoever. Just, you know, he felt so strongly about it, that he wanted to make sure that everyone was aware of some of the issues that were becoming important in applying for medicine and... making sure that everyone's aspirations were raised in the right way, that people knew what they needed to do. It's great: they are meeting twice a week now.

The network of such societies, whereby it was possible to discuss topics in much greater depth than was sometimes possible in lessons (taking them beyond the syllabus as the head of sixth says above), was one of the apparent distinctive features of Merryweather. This does not mean that such discussion did not happen at Carter's, but just that it was not so organisationally developed outside formal lessons. This is significant in relation to the comments made by university admissions tutors in later Chapters.

The societies at Merryweather, and links maintained by senior staff with 'older universities' (ie prestigious), were also key to bringing in outside speakers with an academic focus. The deputy head at Merryweather explains these links, their importance as he sees it and, again, the role of these societies:

... a lot of staff maintain links quite closely, particularly with staff from older universities, but a good Head of Department will very often have links with several universities; we do bring in outside speakers from universities ... we very much encourage that ... Societies ... like the Berkeley Society and Phil

> Soc... (are) bringing in external speakers all the time... so we are doing that
> sort of thing. I suppose you could say we should be doing more... but if the
> whole issue is about aspiration, then part of that must be about lifting your
> sights a bit and realising that it's not just all about the school that you're
> currently in. Bringing in outside speakers does help that.

This work is obviously situated within the drip feed, and 'the whole issue of aspiration', as he says.

Conferences
Both schools held their own conferences and sent their students to outside ones, including ones concerned with university recruitment. The purposes of careers conferences are summed up by the head of careers at Merryweather:

> (Our) careers conference I suppose is the one time in a boy's upper middle
> school and sixth form that they get real exposure to lots and lots of informa-
> tion ... There are about 40 different organisations that will come in, and they
> are all pretty much, 85 per cent of them ... professional occupations. And so
> boys will be able to come in and find out whatever information they want from
> someone who is actually involved in that career.

This comment from the deputy head explains the thinking behind academic- and university-focused conferences, again as part of the drip feed:

> I arrange a medical careers conference for the whole of the ... area, where I
> invite in five or six speakers ... (Students from the surrounding schools) come
> in to hear about what medicine's all about – what its problems are, why
> people like to take it – from a range of speakers, and we give them lunch and
> give them some information ... So those are one-off things, the careers con-
> ference, the medical conference, the (university recruitment) conference...
> and they are little sorts of peaks in the process. But the whole process is con-
> stantly going on through assemblies, through reports ... *Deputy Head,
> Merryweather*

The influence of individual teachers
Parents at both schools often referred approvingly to various named individual members of staff and the positive influence they had had on their children. Sometimes, this was through the role of the tutor: one-to-one feedback was given by tutors at Carter's, for example, during

days when the timetable was suspended. But the role of the tutor was clearly considered important at both schools. The head of sixth at Merryweather explains the role:

> ... the form tutor is the principal pastoral carer and advisor to the lads, although I'm around as the next level up. For the most part they get their information from their form tutor ... And one of the good things about this place is that their form tutor, as well as registering them twice a day, is actually one of their principal teachers ... Their form tutor, as well as register-ing them, will see them in the Chem. lab, or in a History lesson ... so the con-tact between tutor and pupil is very high ... so that is again a constant pro-cess. Some form tutors actually say 'let's ... talk over form period about what your ambitions are' and so on.

The link between subject teaching and tutoring is clearly only possible organisationally with many students studying each subject – the 400 boys in the sixth form at the time of my visit were studying nineteen A Levels between them, plus general studies. But it perhaps also explains the reported strong subject-based influence on the boys by their tutors, affecting university choice, though comments were made also about this at other schools (see Chapter 2). The head of sixth went on to give some examples of the influence of tutors over the pupils' university subject choice, through their subject enthusiasm and 'the fact they could talk about Physics during form periods', as he put it:

> You don't choose your teachers, and some people will get on with some teachers better than others. I couldn't say that there are some teachers who are liked or disliked by everybody, because it turns out that there are different personalities ... Sometimes they do strike a chord with somebody else. How-ever, it is quite clear that there are some teachers who are very inspiring. Their enthusiasm does go over, and therefore the lads say 'I'd really like to do that subject at university'.

This sort of subject influence by named teachers was mentioned by several parents. Merryweather's head of careers explained how this pro-cess worked practically in his sixth form lessons (he was a chemist):

> ... for my typical teaching I have an OHP ... but I keep the board free and it's just called a doodle board. It's a wipe board and we just talk about anything that they want to talk about. If they ask about it, I won't go off the point, any-thing they want to do... so yeah, that is the great strength of being here really.

And further:

> ... so (tutors have) got half an hour then. If there's a problem any time, they can take them out, you know, say 'you don't go to assembly, I won't go to assembly' and talk to them then on a one to one basis if necessary. Again, they are seeing their lads for teaching purposes, and quite often a lad will ask a question during a lesson or before a lesson, and the lesson won't start for another ten minutes because they're talking generally about university choices.

Such flexibility in state secondary schools is unusual in my experience, but that does not mean state schools do not have many inspiring teachers.

How this relates to guidance

Advertising itself as one of the 'academic independent schools', it follows that the existence of academic specialisms, many at PhD level, is seen as important for guidance at Merryweather:

> ...the strength of this place is that I know automatically (that I can say to a boy) 'OK there is an expert in material science in school and go and talk to him, and he will give you as much advice and as much information as he possibly can'... There is... virtually always a contact in school. The guidance community, if you like, spreads wide ... *Head of Careers*

But this does not cover vets, as the reader will recall!

Doing the UCAS form

Completing the UCAS form, in particular the personal statement, is a very important part of the university admissions process. Given that some subjects in some Russell Group universities do not interview candidates unless they are mature or in target postcodes for widening participation funding (see Chapter 5 and 6), it is clearly crucial. Both schools spend considerable time on its completion (and this is recognised by university admissions tutors), but the steady step by step process was most graphically illustrated, again, by the head of sixth at Merryweather:

> ... they take a whole period, which I do in June/July, just before the holidays, and say 'I suggest you get on with this over the summer holiday; it will take several drafts. People who are your best advisors here will be your form tutors, but you know, show it to your parents, show it to your friends', things

like that. They start off by writing something out which is hopeless, and then their form tutors say 'well, where does it actually say that you want to do this because you like this'... they just get guidance, which is not really expertise, it's just common sense. If you've applied to do a particular course, it's how you sell yourself for that, and we just rely on the fact that most of the teachers here are intelligent and they have some ideas about what is being looked for.

Again, this is clearly an important aspect of the 'drip feed which builds and builds', but the normality or everydayness of the staff's understanding of this work takes us back to the fishes in water comment earlier in the Chapter.

The validity of these data

In summary, there is an expected path in these schools which the vast majority of the students are expected to follow. This is regarded as normal for the schools, and many students will have heard it at home. It is reinforced in assemblies, in tutor groups, by tutors, by outside speakers, and in the conferences that students attend. The expectation is underpinned by a process broken down into manageable steps in the schools, which takes the students through thinking about university; choosing what they want to study and where; preparing and making an application, and preparation for additional subject tests where they exist (see the Merryweather head of sixth's comments above on the additional test for Medicine – MMAT – and Chapter 6). There is no escape.

Is this what independent schools in general do? It is not possible to say with complete certainty without visiting a much larger number of schools, but the processes described in this Chapter are echoed in other studies. For example, perhaps somewhat obscurely, the Scottish Independent Schools Project (AERS, 2008) refers to what it calls rituals, such as prize giving and assemblies. But the processes involved in preparing students for university described here are almost a complete match for those at Pugsley's 'Brangwyn Hall' (2003), as 'part of the 'natural' progression in education, from compulsory schooling, to sixth form, to university' (p212). Brangwyn Hall was in south-east Wales, and considering the differences in size, intake, location (150 miles apart), ethos and circumstances of the two schools I visited, it is likely that these processes will be the norm in independent schools – they were found in the state schools which were good at getting students into university, after all (Curtis *et al*, 2008).

This does need some qualification. The independent sector is quite diverse, and includes small faith and other interest schools, as well as the 80 per cent of private school pupils in schools which are covered by the Independent Schools Council, as Geoffrey Walford says in his introduction to his 2003 edited collection. Carter's, Merryweather and Brangwyn Hall belong to this 80 per cent. These are the ones that cater for the natural progression. While about 7 per cent of pupils attend independent schools in England and Wales, this rises to about 10 per cent in London (West and Noden, 2003). But they made up 12 per cent of the first degree intake to all UK universities in 2007/8 (HESA statistics from www.hesa.ac.uk just released at the time of writing), rising to 38.5 per cent at Bristol, 43 per cent at Cambridge and 46.6 per cent at Oxford.

So they do work, and the drip feed processes will be important to their success, but not the sole determinant. How can schools serving predominantly working class or mixed areas take the decision to concentrate on academic routes to university (otherwise the drip feed would not work in assemblies, for example) except by assuming that students with different aspirations will be catered for elsewhere? And if schools wish to cater for all their students effectively, what should the institutional habitus look like?

4

The other contexts of young people's lives: the formation of aspiration as part of identity

... as you go on, you realise that actually a ... lot of what happens to your children is to do with the peer group they end up with, as opposed to... how much influence you as a parent have ... Ann, Carter's

Introduction

The young people featured in these interviews are subject to similar and related expectations from adults in two important social contexts of their lives. At home, proactive parents are keen to ensure the development of an appropriate generic ambition, including a more specific aspiration for university. At school, the staff see their central aim as being to facilitate the university aspiration, as a staging post to professional careers. And this aim, particularly as the school students get older, suffuses school life.

The parents see an aspiration for university as something their children are capable of and therefore a right; the staff consider their work, particularly in relation to preparation for prestigious universities, as completely 'normal' and as it should be. Both sets of adults have described their respective roles in social reproduction, but in terms of an encouraged process of personal development. This is probably how the young people would see their educational trajectory too, should they think about it.

In this Chapter, I consider the other contexts of these young people's lives in the light of the comments made about them by parents and staff. What emerges from these comments is that choice of independent school itself influences these other contexts, but that parents are proactive there too. In the second half of the Chapter, I construct a model for the development of aspiration, from the young person's vantage point, as part of identity.

The other contexts of children's lives: the significance of choosing independent education

Whereas some degree of control is exerted over most aspects of life at home and over formal contacts between staff and students at school, this is more difficult in the other contexts of young people's social experiences, as the responsible adults are absent. These other contexts include the unstructured parts of school life and, therefore, informal encounters with their wider school peer group. Young people may also come across a completely different peer group in their local community, including a different range of adults, if they socialise in contexts outside school friends, or play sport or music. And whom they may come across in their wanderings on the web – from social networking sites to group gaming – is virtually limitless.

These other sources of influence are a worry to all parents. Whatever positive influences may be brought to bear in school and at home, parents may find that other motivations and interests appear in their children from elsewhere. In the interviews, both school staff and parents showed varying degrees of anxiety about other contexts and at the same time a desire to influence them proactively. Such comments arose in the course of discussions about a number of matters, but as there were so many of them, they constituted a substantial theme in the data.

The most important other context is the peer group: primarily the groups of young people children are able to meet and socialise with, because of their circumstances. Ann's comments about the influence of peer group, which headed up this Chapter, echoed the views of other parents. And a number made it quite clear that their choice of a selective independent school involved the conscious choice of a specific peer group for their children, because they perceived them as 'studious', highly able, or academic (echoing West and Noden's 2003 findings). They wanted their children to be with children like them as the following two quotes from Merryweather parents, Kerry and Fay respectively, exemplify:

> ... Then I realised that we had to be careful about the choices of secondary school. The things that he was reading ... we looked around and at some schools I thought 'well, no, J's well beyond this already', so he did need an extra push. It's having other kids who're on the same level as him to discuss books and things ... the same sort of interests, so I think that's why he fitted in here, because there were other boys the same as him.

And:

> ... Since he's been here he has been very happy; he's found a niche here of similar boys: they're all fairly studious and quiet and that's the good thing about (this school), you can find your niche. Particularly once you start your options, you tend to be channelled with kids with the same sort of ... generally similar boys, you know. So he's been alright in secondary school ... but primary school was dreadful for him.

They felt they had made the appropriate choice as these comments show. These statements can also be seen as statements of entitlement and will be considered further in Chapter 6.

However, the choice of independent school also represented influencing the peer group in which they *socialised*. Deborah, with children at Carter's, was one parent who described it as follows, because the students come from a much wider catchment than they would have done at a state school:

> ...coming to an independent school they come from all over the country, and so for kids to socialise out of school hours, they don't socialise in their town or village or wherever they live so much ... A lot of their socialising is in relation to school.

And this echoes what assisted place holders said to researchers funded by the Sutton Trust:

> Independent school pupils tend to be drawn from a relatively large geographical area compared to those attending comprehensive schools ... The workload at independent schools and the often extensive range of extracurricular activities mean that there can be less time for socialising in general. Some respondents found that this had also impacted on their friend-

ships with local children, because they did not get home from school until late, had more homework and were, in some cases, required to attend school on a Saturday. There is also evidence that the schools attempted to protect their pupils from supposedly undesirable or potentially distracting neighbourhood, and even family, influences by providing a near 'total' environment. (Power *et al*, 2009:7)

As if to ram home the message to his sons himself, Adrian, while they were at Merryweather, also exposed them to something different, a classic case of 'the other'. He thought 'you'd be better doing a professional job' and said:

In the summer holidays, both my sons worked for me. The nature of what we do, or did, is with insulation work ... (and so) the people who you are employing are basically at the bottom of the tree ... My sons found it interesting, listening to all their exaggerated stories on a daily basis and their general take on life.

No doubt they discussed it afterwards! Nevertheless, even after controlling for peer group, there were still worries. Despite a selective intake, Ann expressed her academic concerns like this:

... even in schools like this, I still find it sad that there is this phrase 'keeners' around, and you know if you are known to work hard and whatever, there still is this. It's not the right thing, but you don't know how much of it is ... I don't know, I think it will always be around in the peer group and so on, but ... I've been quite surprised by some of the comments that are made by some pupils and I think: 'but hang on a minute, that's why you're at a school like this'...

'Keener' is a south west idiomatic equivalent for such words as 'swot'. She had broader apprehensions:

I even see it particularly interestingly in my daughter's year ... the behaviour of some of the girls in her year group, that she hangs around with ... It's all to do with behaviour of others in the peer group, and it's pure luck really which group she's ended up in.

Other parents at both schools reflected on the inappropriate friends still chosen by their children at certain times. This could variously affect how their children saw the importance of academic work, they felt, and might affect the later emergence of the right sort of aspirations. Deborah again, also with children at Carter's, reflects on the inappropriate choices made by their children at certain times, specifically because of the influence they may have on future trajectory:

> ... there have been a couple of occasions when I have been very concerned about the company the kids have been keeping and I don't know why, but sometimes children do aspire to the lowest common denominator rather than the other direction. And also, with (my daughter) S, when she was top of the lower school and when she first came over to the upper school, she had a little girlfriend whose parents ... were going through difficulties and their daughter was constantly phoning S up for help with homework or cribbing her notes. And S ... was spending hours on the phone in the evening ... I had to then say to the staff 'look, can you please reposition S in the classroom situation, to try and put a bit of space between them, in order that she could make friends with other children'. But also because her neediness was having an adverse affect on S.

A theme begins to emerge from these accounts and the specific instances described. That is, parents act on concerns, or expect the school to do so, sometimes after they have been taken up with staff. This is another perceived complementarity of role. And occasionally, parents described taking matters up themselves with other parents, sometimes when they were not seen in approving terms. Though socialising might be through school peer groups, for example, after sporting fixtures, Deborah showed she did not think this necessarily stopped negative behaviour or influences:

> ...and so one doesn't tend to know the parents so well, and I think it really important for all parents to get to know the parents of other boys because they can't automatically know them ... through other means, when kids want to socialise out of school. I know that several parents have similar concerns...

She expressed her anxiety about the way some of the other parents supervised even quite old children, but nevertheless stated her opinion that even this informal setting was not beyond the school's purview:

> He also was a sportsman ... played rugby and hockey, so it's very interesting that I think perhaps the school may well be able to influence, to have more influence, around the sporting side of things...

Finally on this theme, comments from Lynne, a parent with a son at Merryweather (and one in a state grammar school) exemplified potential parental concerns, action in support of the school (the perceived complementarity of role again), and appreciation of the impact of her son's contacts via the web (though in this case some at least were school peers). This parent was describing what had obviously been a difficult issue for their family to deal with, the details of which are not included here:

> ... There was an incident at school ... so we took his laptop off him; we were quite firm about it and we totally supported the school. That said, there was a bigger incident ... going on. Now ... we talked about it and he said 'I've been done for (——) but I'm really sorry about it' and it stopped. But, that wasn't where it stopped, because these other boys who'd been getting into a lot more serious things... they called him the snitch. And his whole peer group turned on him... By the end of term, he was isolated ... he felt that everybody had daggers for him ... When we went back to school it was still there, and ... one particular Friday night he was on MSN chatting to people that were back from the holiday and so on, and one of the boys had come into the conversation from school and just slated him ... So I took this piece of information: I said, 'Z, can you capture this conversation?' And I took it to Dr T (at Merryweather). ... Anyway, it's been completely squashed; the school were fantastic about it.

So generally, staff were considered to be on the case. In all these cases, the choice of independent school might be seen to extend the parental role by increasing the scope of influence into other social contexts.

In the context of the informal peer group at school, the head of sixth at Merryweather gave examples of peer-generated aspirations which he considered inappropriate, and one of the influences the drip feed (and specifically the role of the tutor) were intended to counter:

> ... however, during the course of the lower sixth-form, peer influence has a tremendous effect. They get into a form, and somebody else says 'what are you going to be? I've got no idea what I'm going to be'. And somebody says 'I'm going to be a doctor', and (so) they think 'well, that's a good idea, I'll be a doctor as well'. So it's that sort of influence. You sometimes find that in some forms: you'll have rather more than you would expect swinging towards one sort of subject; it is peer influence. In some cases inappropriately...

Nevertheless, to be clear, the aspiration mentioned would have been appropriate, involving university and a 'professional job' as Adrian would have described it, even though it may not have suited the individual personally.

Conclusions to draw from these data

Two features emerge from these data which are critical for understanding the managed model of social reproduction. First, the choice of independent school in itself selects peer groups and the social contexts in which young people move, minimising exposure to others. This can be seen as extending the orbit of parenting. But the choice of independent school should also be seen as the choice of particular social (and economic) trajectories; it is not just a school choice thing – this would be misrecognition.

Second, although the choice already begins to minimise the risk to appropriate trajectories, the proactive agency of parents is also critical in minimising even the minimised risk within the independent school settings. It helps Deborah, Lynne, Ann and many others to act on the sorts of worries they expressed. In other words, the proactive strategising we know to be a characteristic of these and other middle class parents' ambitions is at the centre of managing the social reproductive process.

The social process of picking up aspirations

Young people's agency is also important to the functioning of the managed model of social reproduction. They need to take on the generic ambition, develop specific aspirations for universities and professional careers, and act on them knowledgeably for it to work. They need to grow into a view of themselves which includes assumptions of the normality of such aspirations for people like them, and the associated understanding and confidence to achieve them. This is to be their aspirational identity.

The social contexts of these young people's lives are shown in Figure 1 and are represented by the boxes around the outside of the diagram. The arrows show lines of potential influence on the young people and their developing aspirations. Although the extent and the nature of each influence will vary because this is a complex and dynamic network of influence that changes over time, let us consider what we have learned happens in each of these contexts.

In **school**, they are presented from quite early on, as an integral part of their educational experience, with a series of generic ambitions

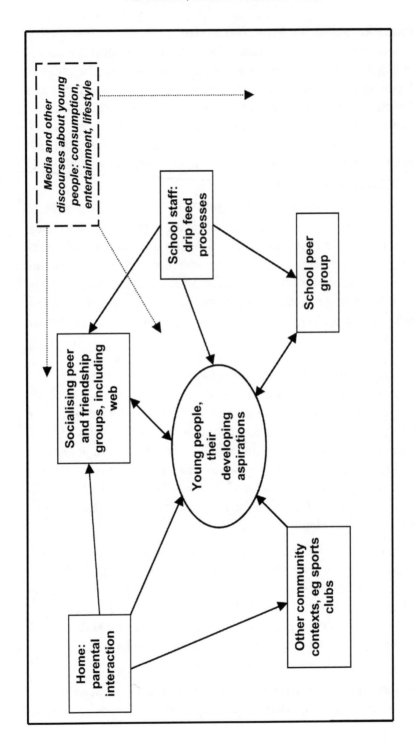

Figure 1: Influences on the development of aspiration

achieved by people like them, ie who used to attend this school, in particular going to a prestigious university and getting professional jobs. Staff talk constantly about university to their students: formally in subject lessons, tutor groups and assemblies; and informally on an individual basis. The message is reinforced by visiting speakers, including alumni, and by events such as the various conferences they attend. The young people receive regular feedback about performance: doing well at GCSE and selecting the right A Levels are related to university entrance and future choice of career. Their paths to university are laid out in a series of micromanaged steps.

Their parents may step in too, for example choosing which university or Oxbridge College to go to, or getting the right work experience placements. Parents may draw on the family's social capital, their wider network of relations, friends and more distant 'loose ties' (Granovetter, 1973). The young people will see more people like themselves in a range of career and university destinations, often, it must be said from these examples, in positions of influence and power. These contacts will work iteratively with the wider networks of their schools, reinforcing habitus.

At **home** itself, these parents, with varying proactivity reinforce the generic ambitions for people like their children, specifically university and a 'professional job' (Adrian). This is through discussion, repeated and revisited many times in some homes, using social capital as just mentioned, and in some cases undertaking joint visits to conferences and universities. These have now reportedly become much more common than ten years ago (see various articles in Times Higher – Swain, 2008 and Feldman, 2008). This is a kind of *domestic* drip feed, which clearly also has 'built and built' for some of the young people.

Two **peer groups** are shown in the diagram opposite: that in school, and others they may come across in socialising, including wanderings on the web, through social networking and gaming. First, we know the school peer group for them is constrained: they will learn with people with 'high ability' similar to them in the academic school climate. Second, we also know that those they socialise with, sometimes at some distance from their homes, and sometimes by involvement in sport, drama or music, are similarly constrained, less directly but just as powerfully.

This peer group, whatever the occasional concerns related by parents, is likely to share similar generic ambitions and self-narratives, as they have gone through similar socially selective processes. As a whole they receive the same set of expectations and experiences at school (and home). The selection of such a peer group (and their parents) is a de-selection of others, consciously or otherwise. Boarding emphasises this even more. But when concerns arise, proactive parent-driven intervention often follows: directly *in situ* with their children, with other parents, with school staff, or all three.

Higher risks to trajectories or reproduction may arise when these young people come across peers in their **community**, who either do not share the same independent school experience, or have not 'received' the transmitted acceptable generic futures. The time available for such contacts is mitigated by school activity-generated social life, however, but is also reduced or made more difficult by the manufactured distinctions of going to independent school – the specific type of school uniform (often including blazer, although Academies seem to be catching up), going to and returning from school at different times, more homework which keeps them in, longer school holidays, the locational and physical nature of the school site, and so on. The Power *et al* (2009) reference above confirms the conscious effort of schools in this regard.

The community contexts mentioned in the interviews also included non-school sporting and drama activities, church, family friends, and social contacts in different settings, in one case a sports club. From the parental descriptions, we know that similar 'people like us' populated these settings. These were milieux framed by the same assumptions of normality, in which the young people will recognise themselves and be like fishes in water. This again minimises the risk of poor influences.

Finally, the young people and their friends will also be exposed to a variety of discourses through **electronic and new media**, reinforced in some social and leisure sites and with friends and acquaintances. These may not mesh entirely with the sorts of generic ambitions envisioned through school, home and immediate family circles and contacts. Young people can become immersed in discourses of consumption, entertainment and lifestyle (Kenway and Bullen, 2008). Such discourses valorise certain assumptions and courses of action or inaction and not others. In figure 1, these are shown in the text box with dotted line sides. Because of the amount of time spent in these places (nearly six hours a day in front of screens, according to ChildWise (2009)), they will contribute dynamically to the habitus with which young people approach and interpret new situations, and hence will suffuse experiences in other contexts.

These discourses are essentially passive, but will provide a set of vocabularies and patterns of thought to express, describe and explain experiences and action, sometimes only to peers, and often through social networking. The question is how different they will be for these young people. Facebook is the most likely networking site to be used given the social origin of these young people: Boyd (2007) and from my own informal experience of working in an organisation that regularly posted on Facebook, Bebo and MySpace. Many – but by no means all – of the young and not so young people using Facebook will be on some stage of a university trajectory, either pre- or post-, and the discourses will have some commonality with those found in other social contexts of the young people's lives. Even with more laconic expression and greater irony, rebellion will be more in form than substance. Consumption, entertainment and lifestyle underpin current ways of living, not challenge them. They are essentially conservative.

The process of learning who I am

So, although this process is not risk- (or anxiety-) free for agency, it as secure as it could be for social reproduction. The young people hear similar narratives in all the contexts of their lives about what is important for people like them, the normality of university and professional career aspirations, what they should spend their time on and how they should behave because of who and what they are.

This is the point of the managed model of social reproduction. At least part of what we think about ourselves involves taking on the expressed views of others about us, especially if by people in socially approved situations that appear normal and where we do not feel like the fish out of water. The self is constituted socially, therefore, at least in part:

> the self ... is essentially a social structure and it arises in social experience... it is impossible to conceive of a self arising outside of social experience. (Mead, 1934:140)

51

This is how habitus develops iteratively. So as our young people move from place to place, and social situation to situation, they begin to absorb these narratives about futures and the discursive practices (Foucault, 1969) in which they are expressed and framed. They begin to see them as part of their destiny, their self-futures, as valorised destinations. Their understanding and experience develop; their dynamically formed habitus recognises and interprets each new one and reinforces itself and the normality of what and who it is. The young people begin to accrete their own stories about themselves, their self-narratives, expressed in the vocabulary and thought structures they have absorbed from the discourses practised in nearly all of the contexts of their lives.

Although the young people may accept these futures with varying degrees of enthusiasm and engagement, according to their parents, they will find it extremely difficult to escape the thought patterns and values of the discourse and find the alternative vocabulary and discourses to rebel fundamentally against them. Other expressions of destiny, and the words and thought processes to express them, are not available to them routinely, and will not appear normal.

And as the school breaks down the understandable and graspable steps to getting into a good university even further, it becomes even more difficult to find a practical, alternative, generic ambition – they develop a generalised feeling that this is right, and will get to know that other people of their age, background and attending schools like theirs 'go to uni'. So moving through school and other social contexts, this understanding develops iteratively and cumulatively. The young people 'come to see the relationships between school, higher education and work' (Ball, 2003a:84) by this process – the function of a discursive practice in Foucault's sense.

This understanding about futures, the self-narrative about trajectories, which for these young people means university and professional job, is their aspirational identity. It develops socially and cyclically like epistemic identity (Pollard with Filer, 1996), and like epistemic identity, it arises in cumulative, dynamic interplay with new experiences encountered or provided and clusters goals, understandings, skills and strategies in dynamic development. Just as progress in epistemic identity (and at school) will vary with the degree of relevance and transferability of young people's learning in all the contexts of their lives (Riddell, 2003), aspirational identity, and its realisation, will depend on the interrelations in destiny narratives between home, school and other contexts, and whether they too are mutually reinforcing or not and are part of a similar discursive practice. If they are not, they may not support, at best, the development of specific aspirations, and at worst, may undermine them.

Summary: born to rule

In this sense, these young people at independent school are born to rule – they are chosen by birth, or at least social circumstances. They have been *preparing all their lives* for prestigious universities and careers. This is the social inverse of 'how working class kids get working class jobs', researched by Phil Willis (1977). The preparation in both cases is by a mutually reinforcing interaction between culture and developing identity, the self-narrative. Willis's lads also knew the broken down steps to achieving what they desired – manual factory jobs with an emphasis on manly, physical labour – but what went on in school was irrelevant except inasmuch as it provided opportunities for manly misbehaviour.

For the independent school students, even the passivity of the consumption/entertainment narratives will be expressed within the social contexts of their lives. They will support and be interpreted through cultural artifacts (posters, clothes, phones, MP3 players) accumulated as part of the young people's 'prosthetic identities' (Skeggs, 2004) and with the wealth they have and expect to acquire. They provide the backdrop for their performing themselves: young people from certain social backgrounds, with certain attitudes to life, who dress and present themselves in certain ways, and who expect to be at university and have a good job. They are working in all these ways to achieve their class positions, as Mike Savage (2000) says. For these young people – and none other in this book – Giddens' 'reflexive project of the self' (1991) is a scaffolded reality of their social circumstances.

Aspirational identity is an aspect of possibly multiple identities, of course, which may express themselves differently in different situations – in a sense it could be seen to fit any or all of Hall's three categories (1992) of identity: the enlightenment, the sociological or the postmodern. Parts of these multiple identities may be conflictual, constituting a greater risk to the emergence of appropriate trajectories, but aspirational and epistemic identity are vital components of social *structure* in the head (see Ball, 2003b), that is, the way that choices of individual, agentic actions are socially constrained; that bring all of us to answer the question 'why do I want to do this now' in a restricted number of ways. Although this represents itself as a process of nurture, personal growth, learning and active choice, it is the process basic to social reproduction.

One of the underpinning processes for recycling social inequality can now be seen to be aspirational identities that differ substantially across society. Although these young people may be prepared for particular educational, occupational and social identities, young people from other social contexts are prepared – and prepare themselves – for quite different ones, like Willis' lads, by the processes which are in their heads. Young people at independent school are prepared for university while working class young people who do achieve it may have it thrust upon them. This is why in the next Chapter, as I begin to apply the notion of aspirational identity to other contexts, it can be seen that working class students require additional personal characteristics to succeed to those which may be possessed by young people at independent schools. Even in this regard, life is easier for young people at independent schools.

5

Those not born to rule: 'aspirant' working class students and higher education

If Britain can seize the opportunities of this new global age, our future is full of potential. Our country will be richer in the years to come. But the ultimate prize will be greater still: the opportunity to create not just a richer country, but a fairer society.

This is the modern definition of social justice: not just social protection but real opportunity for everyone to make the most of their potential in a Britain where what counts is not where you come from but what you aspire to become, a Britain where everyone should be able to say that their destiny is not written for them, but written by them...

And whereas in the past young people were held back by limited chances and limited room at the top, in today's global economy there is no longer a national limit to the number and quality of jobs that will be available to the British people. *Gordon Brown* (Cabinet Office, 2009a, Introduction)

Secure middle class social reproduction but existentially insecure agency

Though the choice of independent school may extend the parenting role and limit the time young people spend in undesirable social contexts, this does not mean the parents feel secure. Their proactive agency, in alliance with the school-micromanaged processes, was considered a necessary feature of the managed model of social reproduction and vital to ensure satisfactory trajectories. But it was beset with doubt.

These snapshots of the workings of social structure reflect other findings. We know from previous studies (eg Ball, 2003a; Power *et al*, 2003; Vincent and Ball, 2006) of major uncertainties at important decision points and transitions in trajectories, such as getting in to the right school or university, and of anxiety as a common component of middle class parenting (Ball, *ibid*).

The reasons for the growth of uncertainty and anxiety among middle class families are not hard to find. The decline of the middle class public and private sector bureaucracies since the 1970s (see Riddell, 2003), and the three major recessions since then, have meant that no one can be assured automatically of a job or career for life, and certainly not one of the same or better quality than their parents, the aspiration of the 2009 social mobility white paper (Cabinet Office, 2009a).

This uncertainty has been heightened by the so-called 'individualisation' of social processes (Lauder *et al*, 2006) – the apparent need for individuals to *make* social structure work for them, as through these parents' proactivity – which is one of the driving factors behind 'credential inflation', real or perceived (Wolf, 2002). And the marketisation of public services has further deepened the vernacular narratives of the citizen consumers battling to get their children in through the increased competition for places at the right schools, and the right universities. Hence the now universal desires of the parents in this book to ensure their children achieve a first degree.

Yet, the objective structures underpinning reproduction for these parents, and their children, is secure, and for them, the task is *maintaining* social position, in some cases using the same institutions as their forbears. The reproductive task is the same for other middle class families, but, if they send their children to state schools, may seem less secure. But even then, if they live in urban areas, their children's schools will be in the higher performing, upper strata of urban school systems (Riddell, 2003), with a narrower social mix skewed upwards, and they will still be in a most advantageous position for their choice of trajectories, including prestigious universities.

In other settings, such as those in market towns or rural areas, there will be a social mix. These schools are most likely to be truly comprehensive (Riddell, 2003; Brighouse, 2003; Newsam, 2003) and, again, to be doing reasonably well in terms of the usual performativity measures – parental over-subscription, league tables, Ofsted inspections and so on. I have come across such schools in consultancy work that commonly boast 80-90 per cent progression post-16 to higher education, while ensuring that other provision for young people, such as vocational, is available elsewhere, often through colleges. So these schools may be regarded as safe for middle class parents too, even though the latter may feel no more existentially secure.

And even if middle class parents send their children to their local, urban comprehensive school with poorer results (for example, see Crozier *et al*, 2008; James and Beedell, 2009), they still do well. The ESRC project from which these publications emerged found that the children of these parents, who may be seen to be acting against their objective class interests by sending them to such schools, still get access to programmes such as that for the gifted and talented described later in this Chapter, even though the schools may not have the assured institutional habitus found in those visited for this book and by Reay *et al* (2005). And prestigious universities, for these students, remained desirable and achieved aspirations.

Working class students

By contrast, students from other, mainly working class, backgrounds are certainly not 'born to rule'. Whereas going to university for middle class students is about maintaining social position, for these students it is about changing or improving it. Working class students will not generally be the objects of constructed parental life projects, or concerted cultivation, as Annie Lareau puts it (2003). And they will certainly experience the same uncertainties of our times, not just in terms of secure and easily available middle class jobs to aspire to, but the availability too of either assured skilled jobs or the manual work looked forward to by Willis' lads (1977).

For many working class students brought up in communities built up historically around major employers, such as a colliery, steel works or large factory, unemployment has persisted for a generation or more, sometimes masked by incapacity benefit claims (Beatty *et al*, 2007). This is particularly so when these communities are away from major conurbations or isolated within them by poor or costly public transport. And the various re-skilling programmes devised from the 1980s by central government have not in themselves attracted the right jobs to these areas, or generated the greater mobility required to travel to where they do exist (Wolf, 2002).

So the aspirational task, developing and achieving an aspirational identity including prestigious university, as distinct from having notions or vaguer dreams about it (Reay *et al*, 2009), involves significant change and upward steps for these students. Most likely, it involves entering games which are new to them. It is not altogether surprising then that the expansion of higher education until the early 2000s was founded on the recruitment of middle class students accelerating at a much greater rate than that of working class ones. The latter did increase, but less rapidly (Ross, 2003; Gilchrist *et al*, 2003; Galinda-Rueda *et al*, 2004). Professional class participation in higher education, on the other hand, where prestigious university is, as we have seen, considered a social right, is now at 'virtually saturation' point (Gilchrist *et al*:78).

The major policy interventions and programmes to encourage a wider social base for participation in higher education, however, which will be examined in this Chapter, were not under way until comparatively recently and will not have affected these figures. The first Sutton Trust summer school, at Oxford, took place in 1997; the Gifted and Talented programmes initiated by Excellence in Cities began in some areas in 1999; and the Excellence Challenge process, the forbear of today's Aim-Higher, commenced in 2001.

Aspirational identity in working class schools and communities

The social structural barriers to the emergence of an aspirational identity in working class students including prestigious university can be understood by applying the framework considered in the last Chapter, reconfigured here with reference to a different social context. Figure 2 includes the intended and possible results of programmes and policy interventions, once university has been raised as a possibility in the mind of the student, but these will be discussed later in the Chapter.

Aspirations for students from working class backgrounds develop through the same iterative social process as those from any other. The

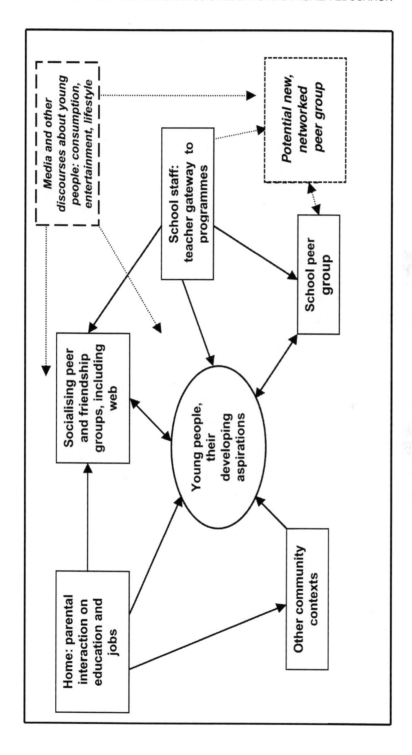

Figure 2: Influences on the development of aspiration in working class communities, represented by arrows

young person takes on the narratives, and discursive practices in which they are framed, about people like themselves and what they are capable of, framing and interpreting them via their developing habitus, and adopting, rejecting, amalgamating or developing them.

At home: parental interaction

Most of these young people are unlikely to be disengaged from family, peers, communities and all the expectations expressed towards them (these extremely vulnerable young people are considered in Chapter 7). The norm is that they are loved and well cared for by their parents, who, while not necessarily having qualifications themselves beyond 16 or 18, consider education important and a potential route for their children to get on. They are generally supportive of teachers and schools, even though they see their children's educational experience as being quite different from their own, which they do not necessarily recollect as positive or relevant.

They may also be aware of the proximity of a university in their home town or city, but do not yet see it as 'recognisably part of their own world and a place where they could feel a 'sense of belonging'' (Raphael Reed, *et al*, 2007:210), particularly if there has been no experience of it in their families. These parents may be extremely pleased that their children are identified at school as potential university attenders. But, nevertheless, although they discuss with their children what they did at school and listen to what the teachers say about exams, discussion at home will not generally be about suitable choices of professional career for 'people like them' after a good university, however positive and supportive these discussions may be. Reay *et al* (2009) found that, for some of the students at 'Southern' (prestigious) University, it was difficult to discuss university life with their parents at all as it was so 'other'.

Other community contexts

These parents may also have a rich network of family, social and work contacts (some of which may be Granovetter's 'loose ties' – 1973), but few will boast the sort of social contacts claimed by parents in Chapter 2, who were smartly enrolled on behalf of their children. They will not generally know someone in Rothschild's, for example, to help arrange work experience for one of their children who may want to be a merchant banker, and they may not have thought of it anyway. It is unlikely, though not impossible, they will have a godfather who is a Cambridge professor, and whose advice they could use to challenge that being given by the school, if indeed any is given at all. Even if they did know such people, it is unlikely that they would be able to ask the right questions and relate them to steps in possible trajectories for their children. Nor are they likely to have many friends with whom they could knowledgeably mull them over. So, although these parents do engage with education and what it might mean, they will do so on different terms.

Other working parents will not be able to do this much. The circumstances of some of the parents, for example because of extreme poverty or drug dependency, will be such that they will find it difficult to engage effectively with their children or their schools, or indeed any other institutions or services. This will also affect their children's trajectories.

Socialising peer and friendship groups

The children identified by their teachers as potential university attenders may be lucky to have a sibling similarly identified, to provide some mutual support, or they may be going through these processes largely by themselves when out of school. Surveys and studies of young people in some working class communities show it is assumed normal and reasonable to pursue jobs and careers not requiring a degree, or even any qualifications, and to have no aspiration beyond achieving similarly to their parents (Watts and Bridges, 2006; SHM, 2004; Archer, 2003), no matter what their teachers think of them or say.

So the young person who has begun to think about university because of experiences at school, or because they have begun to think about a particular career (Reay *et al*, 2009), or for other reasons, as many of them seem to do (Atherton *et al*, 2009), may be surrounded by friends and peers, including relatives, at school and in the community, who have other aspirations which are more normal for them. Further, with the potential doubts about going to university highlighted in parts of the above studies and Raphael Reed *et al* (2007) – potential debt, whether I am able enough, whether I will fit in – students must also be able to resist the easy money available in some areas, such as the Bristol South constituency, from unskilled – but insecure – employment.

Although some do so, developing and maintaining an aspirational identity including university, in the face of different expectations from peers and acquaintances, requires some special determination, or resilience as Raphael Reed *et al* put it. Again, this determination comes through Reay *et al*'s interviews (*ibid*). A critical factor for the iterative development of aspirational identity is that most of the peer group context in school and outside for these students will not be seeking university destinations or graduate employment, and such matters will not feature in their conversations and everyday assumptions.

School

The school context has been left until last because it is here that most of the policy interventions of the past twenty years have been focused, either in terms of changing what goes on there, or providing a 'gateway', as it will be called later, to other provision. Because of this, it is not possible to give the sort of authoritative description of state schools serving working class communities that has been possible for independent ones, though of course there will be similarities.

Part of the difference will between be where working class communities are and how big they are. In small towns, or on smaller housing estates bordered by more middle class areas, for example in some suburbs, the local school, again, is likely to have a broader social mix (Riddell, 2003; Brighouse, 2003; Newsam, 2003). This will benefit working class students, giving them access to a broader set of social and educational aspirations where university ambition may be normal for many (Thrupp, 1999).

For young people living in larger working class communities such as those in major cities, or built round the premises of a major employer, the school will have a narrower social mix. The larger the conurbation, the greater will have been the effects of social and market determined stratification (Riddell, 2003, 2007) and the schools will be in the middle or bottom strata of urban school systems.

This will have compositional effects on aspiration. There will be a greater proportion of young people in the schools from families suffering material or social disadvantage, making it difficult to maintain the relationship with school, never mind find a focus on educational, social and occupational outcomes. And even where there is no material or social disadvantage, there may be aspects of the learning disadvantage described in Chapter 1, arising from the dissonance between the learning contexts and expectations in school and home, compounded by differing linguistic and behavioural expectations between peers and between adults and children (Riddell, *op cit*).

Historically in these schools, and before the policy interventions of recent times, this would have meant the schools' provision would have been weighted heavily towards special educational needs and behaviour, with a back up system of segregated special units and schools. Sometimes, it would have been a badge of pride for some staff to concentrate on such needy children at the expense of those we have learned to call gifted and talented. Despite good intentions, and often because of them, institutionally the schools may have offered narrower, more basic-skills focused pedagogies and curricular experiences (Haberman, 1991; Thrupp, 1999; Riddell, 2003). This is Haberman's so-called Pedagogy of Poverty. A weighting towards literacy and numeracy will perforce present narrower educational, social and occupational horizons to young people as reasonable for (people like) them. And the same emphasis in the national literacy, numeracy, Key Stage 3 and later, national, strategies, developed since the mid-1990s, will have had the same effect.

Ofsted's first report on urban education (Ofsted, 1993) found what it diagnosed as low teacher expectations to be one of the major causes of poor attainment and aspiration. This continues to be identified as a factor by recent studies, such as Raphael Reed *et al* (2007). Where there are low expectations, these will be compounded by the (anti-)keener culture referred to by Ann, a parent at Carter's (see p44). In other words, an anti-achievement or anti-learning culture will predominate in substantial proportions of the peer group and mean that doing well – and being pleased with it – would need to be masked.

Also more recently, several interviewees for this research described working with teachers who did not know how to advise on progression to, and preparation for, university. Whatever the actual expectations of their students, they did not know enough about either the current breadth and scope of higher education, or the processes and requirements for getting into prestigious universities:

It varies from place to place, school to school. It is hard. It's hard too to get (teachers) to understand that HE is a very different place now to twenty years ago when they were in HE ... there are many different routes now to accessing HE, many different courses, some of them delivered in FE colleges. The kids we're looking for are no longer just the top fifteen percent, so we're looking now at a much larger spectrum; there's a much more diverse provision. *Susan, AimHigher Coordinator*

So all those sorts of things are built in to (our work) because it's an information gap, and often their teachers don't know either and that's the thing: (students)'re not getting advice at school because the teachers are just not in a position to give that advice. *Tamsin, educational charity*

This latter comment is in contrast with the independent schools, where the links maintained with prestigious universities were considered important for students' eventual progression there.

Finally, even when young people's aspiration for prestigious universities has begun to emerge in such schools, they are unlikely historically to have had the relentless drip feed process in place identified in independent schools, but some may do so now. Andy Curtis (Curtis *et al*, 2008) and his colleagues, in a study commissioned by the Sutton Trust, found that schools serving working class or disadvantaged communities (identified by free school meals entitlement) which were good at fostering progression to prestigious universities did have such processes, particularly post-16 as has been said. But these schools were extremely difficult to identify.

So overall, for working class students attending working class schools, if aspirations begin to emerge for prestigious (or any) universities, whether in school or because of an interest in a particular career (Reay *et al*, 2009), historically it will have been very difficult for them to develop as the fully blown, self-assured aspirational students found in independent schools. The young people do not routinely encounter the narratives of such aspirations being normal for them in any of the social contexts of their lives. And some of the historic problems continue to persist.

Intervention to raise aspirations: narratives, assumptions and their consequences for policy

Addressing 'poverty of aspiration' as David Blunkett, a former Secretary of State for Education, referred to it (2000), has been an important policy aim since the early days of the Labour Government elected in 1997. The quotation from the current Prime Minister which heads this Chapter, taken from his introduction to the social mobility white paper to be discussed in Chapter 8, touches on two important policy narratives which occur again and again in government documents.

The first narrative is about globalisation. Globalisation offers many new opportunities to us in the UK, according to the Government, including emerging markets in which we can compete on our strengths such as personalised and financial services, and which will enable more access to skilled and high paying jobs. At the same time, the opportunities are balanced with challenges. Emerging markets are in countries with emerging economies, such as those in China and India, which expect to compete with the West in the future on more than basic manufactured goods. And even before considering the high numbers of skilled graduates produced by Chinese and Indian university systems every year, there is a major skills gap now between the UK and its major competitors, which must be bridged to maintain the UK's position. The gap, as measured by levels of qualifications, was identified by the Leitch Report (HM Treasury, 2006), the words of which have now entered standard usage across the wider public and private sectors. Overall, the expectation is that there will be fewer jobs at lower skilled levels and more at higher. Hence the need to adapt.

One of the skills gaps to be bridged is at first (bachelor's) degree level. 'Leitch', as it is often referred to, set a target of 40 per cent of the UK adult population having a degree-equivalent qualification by 2020 (or at so-called Level 4 as it is referred to in the UK). Tony Blair, in his speech to the Labour Party Conference in 1999, had voiced a Government aspiration of 50 per cent of 18-30 year olds having begun a degree by 2010, and Leitch considered this to be a useful staging post to 2020. This is why the further expansion of higher education continued to be seen as an important policy goal.

The second policy narrative in Gordon Brown's quotation – achieving social justice – follows from the first. Moving from a small minority attending university (less than 10% before the Second World War – Archer, 2003), to in effect half the cohort, requires recruitment from wider social backgrounds than ever before, particularly as the expansion of the 1990s catered predominantly for the middle classes. So more young people from working class backgrounds need to go to university. But it is also a matter of justice that they do so.

This second narrative too is commonly found in Government documents, but is also widely shared across the public, private and voluntary sectors: across higher education, as my interviews with admissions tutors shows, and by a variety of educational charities, some of which are associated with well-known philanthropists and businessmen. Of the educational charities, perhaps the best known has been the Sutton Trust, which among other things, supported the first summer school at Oxford, as has been said, for year 12s (17 year olds) who might not have thought of applying there. The trust has also published papers and research reports for some time on a variety of contentious topics, such as social mobility. Other organisations include the Ogden Trust, the Brightside Trust, and a variety of more locally-based charities, which often make grants available to individual talented students.

Realising these narratives requires making some further assumptions. First of all, that many people who in the past did not go to university could have done so if they had had the opportunity. In practice, this implies that their pre-university qualifications could have been higher if only the school system had done the right thing by them. And second, if they were sufficiently high, or even if they were not, not going to university was a matter of aspiration. Hence appropriate policy interventions would concern themselves with discovering previously unrecognised talent, ensuring it is rewarded with the right qualifications, and raising the expectation in those potentially newly qualified that they should progress to university. The nation's future prosperity depends on it, the narrative goes; as we have discovered, the social process required is the capacity across much wider strata of society to construct and support aspirational identities that include university.

National policy interventions for raising aspirations

In one sense, much of the policy activity over the past twenty years could be seen to contribute to discovering unrecognised talent and raising the nation's skills and higher education games. All the programmes for raising standards could be included: the strategies referred to earlier, the development of a national system of school inspection, urban interventions such as Excellence in Cities, Academies, specialist schools, and a variety of policies to tackle low attaining schools and/or ones in so-called challenging circumstances, such as the most recent National Challenge (DCSF, 2008b). The effects of all these various interventions are contested, and have been much discussed elsewhere (Riddell, 2003, 2005, 2009, and many other authors), and so not much more will be said about them here. Their success or otherwise – and those of many minor or geographically specific activities, for example, non-systemic, strategic ones sustained by charities – form the policy climate for the two major interventions specifically intended, first, to develop and bring on a stream of top performing students from circumstances where it might not have existed before, and, second, to promote access to higher education from social strata unrepresented there in the past. If the policy climate has produced high-aspirational schools with rising attainment, then the two interventions are most likely to be soundly rooted. If it has not, then they will not be.

The two interventions in England which will be discussed are the programmes and activities for gifted and talented students and the Aim-Higher programme. These interventions could potentially change, if successful, the structural relationship between social background, higher education and social and occupational trajectory. Or at least, this is their field of operation.

However, it is also necessary later to consider briefly what may be considered broader social interventions, such as the Every Child Matters programme with its five outcomes – see DfES (2004) and DCSF (2007) – and including the extended schools programme (DfES, 2005b), as they may contribute to helping root gifted and talented provision and Aim Higher in the non-school contexts of young people's lives.

The two national policy interventions in England at the time of writing (2009) were overseen by central government departments. The exact typology does not matter as it has changed several times over the past few years and is likely to do so again. But a critical point is that more than one department is involved, more than one national funding body, and that institutions operating the interventions may be funded from more than one source to undertake related work. Also, unlike other government programmes in the past, none of this work is subcontracted as a whole to the private or voluntary sector, though organisations in both may support or be involved nationally or locally.

Gifted and Talented Provision
The arrangements

Provision for gifted and talented students – the words 'National Programme' began to creep into the discussion from 2008 (DCSF, 2008c) – is now expected to be made in all schools, although apparently one in five primary schools claim they have none, according to senior officials (Maddern, 2009b). The word provision will be used for the rest of this Chapter.

The term gifted and talented first appeared in connection with one of the strands of Excellence in Cities, a compulsory urban education initiative (DfEE, 1999) first launched in six major conurbations, and gradually rolled out to the extent that much smaller urban areas in the midst of large counties (e.g Norwich) were able to have Excellence Clusters, albeit with less funding and reduced programmes (see Riddell, 2003:131-134 for a fuller description of the earlier stages of this work). The new term gifted and talented signalled a new policy initiative and began to replace terms in common usage such as 'more able' and 'very able' from the late 1990s – for example, see Freeman's review for Ofsted (1998). Nevertheless, some of the LAs visited for this book used hybrid terms such as 'able, gifted and talented'.

The organisation, management and oversight of gifted and talented provision have been subject to change over a ten year period. The few local authorities receiving the originally earmarked funding were able to employ coordinators at LA level, often responsible to partnership arrangements with schools, and pay for staff time in schools to co-ordinate the work, often as a member of the leadership team. The funding has been gradually devolved to schools and has stopped being earmarked. LAs which had formally employed coordinators, usually in urban areas, commonly absorbed them into other LA teams with varying titles – national strategy, secondary transformation and so on.

One of the original expectations of the DCSF (the DfEE at that time) was that schools identify a cohort of between 5 and 10 per cent of their roll, irrespective of schools' overall attainment. It was the progress of this cohort which was to be monitored. Identifying the cohort remains important at school level, but there has been a National Register of gifted and talented students since 2006, and this is now picked up, literally, through the annual electronic pupil census. A far greater percentage than 10 per cent of young people have benefited from the provision in some schools, as the gifted and talented coordinators interviewed for this research testified.

A National Academy for Gifted and Talented Youth (NAGTY) had been founded to identify, and make national and regional provision for the top 5 per cent of the national cohort, and develop and promulgate good practice. These two strands were sundered in 2007, however, and Warwick University decided not to be involved. Instead, Young, Gifted and Talented was set up and run by CfBT, a not-for-profit organisation. Its provision – through the Learning Academy – can be seen from its website. Password access to it is self-decided by young people, so long as they have been identified as gifted and talented by their school. Use of the Learning Academy is now intended to be monitored at school, not LA, level as was formerly the case.

This provision is to be developed further following policy announcements in 2009, with the availability of an online 'catalogue of opportunities' available at LA, regional and national levels, reflecting a better developed hierarchical network of partnerships compared to ten years ago. See DCSF news for 28 July, 2009 (www.dcsf.gov.uk) and Maddern (2009a) for details of these announcements. They further included an annual scholarship for students from deprived backgrounds 'to help them develop their particular gift or talent' (DCSF news, above), a new category of 179 already-identified and to-be-funded specialist schools for Gifted and Talented, with responsibility for developing and supporting provision in other schools, and an expansion of the City Gates scheme designed to encourage young people entitled to free school meals to go to university.

Identification

The stakes are high for getting the identification of gifted and talented students right. Not only will they have access to new and interesting curriculum activities, they will potentially be able to walk through the 'teacher gateway', as an AimHigher Coordinator described it, to all national and local provision encouraging wider progression to higher education. Yet nearly all the gifted and talented coordinators I interviewed, and the senior government officials, still described identification as 'work in progress', despite nearly twenty years of discussion and advice about the 'more able'.

After the launch of the Excellence in Cities strand, identification began with the use of data from national curriculum tests and the variety of additional general screening tools used by schools, such as MidYIS (the middle years information system) and Cognitive Ability Tests (CATs). These were supplemented and sometimes checked by teacher nomination.

In practice in secondary schools, with nomination by subject teachers, but the definition of gifted being 'learners who have the ability to excel academically in one or more subjects such as English, drama, technology' (DCSF, 2008c:1), some students would be nominated in some subjects only and not included in the formal cohort. Such students would be put on the 'shadow register', a term widely in use at the time of the interviews, and would sometimes benefit from extra provision. 'Talented', incidentally, describes 'learners who have the ability to excel in practical *skills* (my emphasis) such as sport, leadership, artistic performance, or in an area of vocational skill' (DCSF, *ibid*).

But the desire to get it right had led not unnaturally to some of the co-ordinators interviewed, except in newly set-up Excellence schemes, beginning to supplement data and teacher nomination with that by peers and parents. A regional coordinator, in a 2005 interview, gave the example of a student whose school attendance had slipped to about 30 per cent by year 9 and was therefore receiving the school's attention for the wrong things; indeed, he was not known by gifted and talented staff. But he had been running his own music-related website for two years, known and used by his peers, and was making money from it. He was included in the cohort.

In fact, so inclusive was the approach in this coordinator's large area, that he considered that:

> ... the provision itself (could be seen as) an identification tool. For a lot of students, they're never going to know themselves what they could be any good at, because no one's ever given them the opportunity to discover whether they are any good at it or not. So the idea behind a lot of our provision is actually, you provide it as a beginning point, and then you begin to evaluate whether that hit the audiences that it needed to hit. And then you provide it again in a more streamlined way. *Steve, Regional GT Coordinator*

This broad inclusiveness could be seen as inspiring, especially if previously unidentified students are sufficiently motivated by their involvement to then undertake and sustain a more concentrated programme of work (and attainment) in order to go to university. These cases might be rare, but the professional unease felt was about whether all those young people who have the ability to excel, as the Government puts it, are picked up either through their high attainment, or through demonstrating high levels of so-called general or cognitive ability through the CATs or other scores, in the absence of the former, or teacher nomination.

CATs scores themselves are the result of a sort of performance under certain conditions, of course, and it remains an open question whether cognitive or general ability or intelligence either exists beyond measured performance at certain times or indeed whether it is the driver of all other performances, including academic. We know some gifted and talented practitioners do believe this though: see Strand (2006) and the comments made by Radnor *et al* (2007) about the teachers they worked with. But we also know scores vary for individuals and that globally, intelligence quotients have been rising for some time.

It seems important that screening continues to take place, and developments such as the more sophisticated approach to primary school data I learned about in a 2009 interview, based on the new national progress tests, intended to be used to test children's progress by national curriculum levels. New young people may continue to be identified in all these ways.

But it is also essential that not being identified through screening is not seen by teachers as a once and for all ontological judgment – you either have this key driver, or not; you have ability, or not – because this will affect the self-narratives being considered here once and for all, and will deny access to future opportunities, much like the IQism discussed by Gillborn and Youdell (2000). And as far as teacher nomination is concerned, teachers must keep an open mind, like Steve, to the possibility of catching an unexpected glimpse of some of their students' potential during an unexpected activity, which might engender at a particular time that peculiar self-reinforcing concatenation of previously unseen motivation, interest and actual performance.

And if teachers really are to have an open mind, they need to have an open mind about the behaviours and performances they may only glimpse infrequently in a student's time with them. If they believe in the notions of general and fixed ability, as many clearly do, they may translate this, for example, into the capacity to reason, think abstractly and solve problems in certain ways. Culturally, the danger is that they may instinctively pick up on these sorts of behaviours – perhaps ways of talking, showing interest and engagement, or being bright or quick (Ball, 2003a) – to the exclusion of all others and the students who exhibit them. But these behaviours are part of the normal narratives of middle class families and students, as will be discussed in the next Chapter, and are similar to the attributes sought by at least the prestigious universities. Some working class students will therefore need induction into them, it will be argued, before they can display them, and it is what might precede the demonstration of these behaviours, and how they are socially constructed in their classrooms, that teachers need to be alive to if they are to be inclusive.

Parental and peer nomination need to remain.

New provision

Although the curriculum and pedagogy for gifted and talented students, previously mostly referred to as the more able, have been developing for at least twenty years in England, there are two developments in the overall policy intervention for gifted and talented which are critical for the social processes involved in developing aspirational identity.

The first is the development of a cohort, or group, of gifted and talented students in school itself, who may know and work with each other. The second is the great flowering since national funding became available of new collaborative enrichment activity. This makes it possible for members of the cohort to meet peers from a wider group of schools and communities and, sometimes, nationally, through the work of the former NAGTY, the Learning Academy and soon from the online catalogue.

Excellence in Cities funding provided the time to put on such activities at local, regional and national levels, and to do the essential follow up back into school and classrooms. Organisations such as London Gifted and Talented – part of the London Challenge (see Riddell, 2003 and www.londongt.org) – have enabled an extraordinary range of such activities, often focused on real contemporary topics of interest, such as the development of Crossrail, undertaken with the people responsible for them in real life.

And although the reinforced emphasis in the 2009 announcements was on progress to university, LA Gifted and Talented Coordinators I interviewed described and sent me details of work they had organised previously themselves, or managed access to, in connection with possible university attendance, and described some of the expectations of follow-up in school (often referred to as 'key'). Some projects were innovative and exciting, including campaigns through the local media and web information for parents (see ST19, for example, in South Tyneside).

In some areas, the LA coordinator interviewed was both the Gifted and Talented Coordinator and the AimHigher Coordinator, but more usually these were separate posts, partly because of the different ways the two programmes were originally set up, with different funding arrangements and target groups, and covering different geographical areas. Even where the posts were distinct, however, the holders were often in touch with each other and sometimes were based in the same or neighbouring offices. The moving together of these programmes nationally had been occurring locally for some time.

Class composition of the gifted and talented cohort

Unlike AimHigher, Gifted and Talented has not historically been organised to target working class students per se, although this may be changing with the emphasis on City Gates in the 2009 announcements. Direct evidence that middle class students were benefiting from the provision has been mentioned (James and Beedell, 2009; Crozier *et al*, 2008), but this was inevitable from the way that Excellence in Cities schemes were set up to begin with. They included affluent urban schools in the major conurbations in phase1 and 2 of the scheme, with students who came with some of the advantages described in the last Chapter.

These students, albeit a small minority in some of the original LAs to receive funding, would be given access to the teacher gateway, in figure 2, and would share some of the advantages of the independent school students at home and in some of the social communities in which they mixed. They may also benefit from access to the new more networked peer group also shown in Figure 2 to be discussed shortly.

These students should not be overrepresented in the gifted and talented cohorts – as national officials and Gifted and Talented Co-ordinators interviewed said, and the national guidance (DCSF, 2008c) makes clear – but they will be competing well. Several coordinators des-cribed work they had done in schools to help achieve a more balanced cohort representative of the school's roll, but we just do not know the social origin nationally of the students involved, even though schools are expected to act on it to ensure a balanced cohort. The original evaluation of Excellence in Cities (Kendall *et al*, 2005) included no data at all on this.

Sustainability and spread

This flowering of collaborative activity has been made possible with new funding, but much of this is now devolved by central government to local government and schools. Outside opportunities, as opposed to the everyday activities in school which need to be sustained and paid for, have always been difficult to protect in schools experiencing budget pressure, and where they require partnership activity, which is costly in time, effort and therefore money. These activities, therefore, are poten-tially vulnerable even in those areas which have received funding in the past, no matter what schools, LAs and regional partnerships think of them. For developing aspirational identity, as can be seen from Figure 2, it is crucial that they be repeated and sustained.

The sorts of exceptionally exciting enrichment activities described in this research have never been available nationally. I learned on a 2006 visit to a school serving a market town and rural area that nothing was provided in this high-performing LA, and the limited enrichment provision between schools was managed and run by them from their own budgets, on their own initiative. Sustaining any aspiration once aroused, therefore, would depend even more on schools and teachers, even when the teacher gateway was wide open, positive and looking out for unsuspected flares of potential.

AimHigher
Origins and funding
The other national policy intervention, AimHigher, was specifically intended to increase the number of young people from disadvantaged backgrounds having the qualifications and aspirations necessary to enter higher education. It emerged from the combination of the Excellence Challenge – another Excellence in Cities activity launched in 2001 – and Partnerships for Progression, a consultation for which was launched by HEFCE and the Learning and Skills Council (LSC) in December of the same year, intended to help form the most effective partnerships between schools, further education colleges and higher education.

The unified AimHigher programme is now managed by the funding bodies for higher education and post-16, and is overseen currently (2009) by two government departments. AimHigher partnerships include higher education institutions, schools, LAs, training and further education providers, and 'other partners and stakeholders' (from www. aimhigher.ac.uk), typically from business and community organisations. The partnerships cover all English (government) regions, with more local area partnerships: for example, there are three in the south west.

Although funding was originally announced for only three years, it has been gradually extended until 2011. Funding is held centrally by the partnership, and locally by universities, colleges and schools. Typically, there will be a 'lead HEI', where the regional coordinator is based, but individual higher education institutions take the lead on particular matters or pieces of work where they have specific expertise or interest.

Targeted activity

AimHigher has been highly targeted by the use of sophisticated Intervention Models (for example, see Anderson *et al*, 2005), based on generally lower attainment and neighbourhoods 'with lower than average HE participation' for schools, and additionally, area deprivation data for colleges. This particular model cited places schools and colleges into four bands which determine the level of AimHigher activity available: the more deprived, the more activities can be accessed. Originally, the target group was aged 13-30, but AimHigher has supported activities for younger students than that.

The range of activity undertaken under AimHigher is considerable, according to one earlier 'opportunities prospectus' (AimHigher West Area Partnership, 2005). The stated intentions are to raise awareness and aspirations, help schools and colleges raise attainment, and ensure young people are 'fully informed' (p7), in order to ease transition to HE. Schools and colleges are expected to identify their 'widening participation cohorts' and then choose appropriately from the activities which may be made available to them by AimHigher.

Just as the identification of gifted and talented students has broadened and become more flexible, the criteria for schools and colleges to consider in the south west for the widening participation cohort are also broader than numerical proxy measures such as postcode information and free school meals entitlement. The criteria are available in a number of places, including the opportunities prospectus just mentioned, but see also www.aimhighersw.ac.uk/cases/casestudy11.htm, accessed 11 May 2009). Institutions are exhorted to consider 'learner specific information', including about the individual and their family (p2 of this case study). This may be their socio-economic status, and family and personal circumstances.

Activities available through AimHigher have included school- and university-based presentations and sessions on the various facets of going to university – what you need to do if you want to go, finance, university life and what it is like being a student. These are run both by university staff and student ambassadors, who are current under-graduate students, sometimes from the same communities as those they are working in. Some of the visits to universities can begin as young as year 6 in primary. All of these might be described as both awareness and aspiration raising. A variety of subject based activities are arranged, including masterclasses, revision and enrichment sessions, and taster sessions or days where a group of students may spend time in a univer-sity lab, for example, doing university science.

There are parallel sessions for parents and carers to provide informa-tion about higher education, finance, and what they can do to support their children in applying for a place and working towards it.

There is a range of summer schools, both residential and non-residen-tial for students, which begin after year 11 and go through to year 12. These AimHigher ones are targeted, and by this stage are for 'dis-affected' students who could make it to university, but may not do so on current performance for various reasons. These complement summer schools run by other organisations such as the Sutton Trust and some run by universities themselves with their own funding.

Finally, to aid students in plotting their way through these activities, planning a coherent programme, and developing trajectories to higher education, student mentors are available to give one to one support to the students themselves. By this stage in a student's trajectory (typically key stage 4), this is more about sustaining than raising aspiration.

The following extract from an interview with a widening participation officer at a Russell Group university provides a practical illustration of mentoring and how it might fit in to the wider programme of aspiration raising. He draws from his own experiences:

> ...if the mentoring relationship works well ... when (it) develops, what we'd hope is that it broadens the young person's horizon. So even if (university) wasn't something on their agenda before, it would then be something they would contemplate ... When the programme started I actually did mentoring for a year myself so I could get a sense of what it was like ... The young person I worked with didn't really have a good impression in the sense of what university or higher education was about, but as the relationship

developed we began to explore career options and what things we could do ... That was what began to open up his mind. And for us in the mentoring programme, we'd hope that because there were those widening participation cohorts who would have been identified earlier, they would have been doing some of the other activities with student ambassadors. They wouldn't in a sense then be so unfamiliar to them that by the time they got to the mentoring intervention, they would have visited a university already, know something about it. *William, Widening Participation Officer*

Critical success factors
Identification of the AimHigher cohort is important for its success and increasing the stream of non-traditional students to higher education. According to AimHigher staff interviewed, this is primarily a matter for teachers, so the nature of the teacher gateway is important. But once identified, how activities come together coherently for the individual student is also critical, both those selected for them by the school and those chosen themselves, for example from the learning academy or online catalogue. For aspirational identity, what matters is how an aspiration is first aroused in young people, for whom it may not have been natural socially, and how these widened horizons are then iteratively sustained and enriched in the various social contexts of their lives, including those of the national programmes themselves.

Creating coherence for the individual student: how the national policy interventions could work
Increasing intensity
Modelling the national policy interventions at their best, they are likely to come together most effectively in an urban school which has received maximum funding in recent years, has developed a pedagogy and provision in the curriculum for gifted and talented students, and sends students to collaborative activities developed for them. Because of where it is and the social circumstances of the communities it serves, the school has the highest level of AimHigher activities available, and benefits from a range of complementary one-off programmes provided by employers, universities (such as aspiration days at one top university) and other projects such as Education Action Zones and the New Deal for Communities. To ensure this is coherent for its students, instead of a series of apparently unrelated activities, the school will have provided senior

management time and a salary allowance to manage its involvement. From the young persons' points of view, it may work as follows.

They experience a *managed series* of higher education exposures, increasing in intensity as they get older, and intended to raise their aspirations gradually for university. The students come across university academics working in their classrooms on an enrichment basis in the top years of primary school. Once in secondary, and identified as gifted and/or talented, they attend workshops provided by sixth form gifted and talented students. They attend masterclasses given by academics and others, and experience a greater variety of enrichment activities in school, complementing the rest of their timetable and extending them and making them think. They meet a student ambassador (from a similar ethnic or community background), from whom they hear about aspects of university life, surviving once there and critically what they need to do to get there. They visit universities for one-off activity days, where they are taught in the university environment. As they get older, and have been identified as students who could go to university, but will not do so on current form, they are assigned a student mentor, again from a similar ethnic or community background.

As this is all going on, the students are attending gifted and talented enrichment activities run collaboratively between schools, some of which will relate to higher education possibilities. These will have become repeated and progressive parts of their experience, making success in learning seem compelling, convincing and achievable, because it has been done before by people like them whom they've now met. The students begin to see the steps they must take themselves and understand what they need to do. University is becoming a developing and more rooted part of their aspirational identity, and the activity is becoming an important (and unexpected) source for them of new excitements and potential aspirations. They meet a wider group of young people from similar and different backgrounds, from a wider geographical area, but with cognate developing aspirations and plans. University is becoming a usual part of their conversations and daily thoughts. Some of the major reasonable fears about university, for example, finance (Archer *et al*, 2003; Watts and Bridges, 2006), begin to be allayed by these experiences and AimHigher briefings and the students begin to see ways through them.

A different peer group

Susan, an LA Gifted and Talented Coordinator at the time of her interview, gives a flavour of such collaborative activity and explains how they may begin to see themselves differently in this context:

> ... I (do) think they see themselves differently. They develop a new peer group, friendship group. In schools they nurture ... – it's a G & T coordinator who generally (does this) – ... these youngsters and they provide opportunities ... If we get it right, they're mixing across schools ... Parents are saying one of the things they value is their child mixing with children from different schools ... Over the years they are coming together, you know, only for short periods and so on, but they are comfortable mixing with people they don't know. They are very comfortable in that environment. That's a social skill ... I think that's really important. If they're not confident and comfortable in unusual environments, they're going to fall apart ... in front of an Oxford tutor ... It is the small regular events like the debates after school where we have the clusters of schools getting together. So we now have ... groups of ... hugely different schools ... And those kids do now know each other ... (and) go round ... every half term ... to a different school for a debate or something (else) ... They get to know each other. They have critical thinking evenings and ... I think the impact of that is social: they mix. We always consciously mix them up, they never work in school groups...

This is a clearly expressed version of a claim made by a number of gifted and talented coordinators and government officials. A number of interviewees, including Susan, said that, after a variety of these events involving students from more than one school, and national and regional events run by the former National Academy, they observed the routine exchange of mobile phone numbers.

So it is possible that young people identified as part of the Gifted and Talented and AimHigher cohorts may begin to develop an additional peer group to the ones that may have been natural for them (see Figure 2). The school and socialising peer groups with non-university or academic aspirations may have begun to be supplemented by this new, networked one, shown in dotted lines. Facilitated electronic contact after these collaborative events may make it possible for there to be an increased aspirational virtual community of peers, reinforced by repeated contact. This will overlap with the school-based peer group, and attending collaborative events with a peer or friend from school is always easier.

School Processes

Back in school, the expectation expressed by Susan, Steve and other Gifted and Talented coordinators was that the school Coordinator continue to target the young people concerned and those who taught them (ie to maintain the aspiration), particularly with regard to agreed targeted outcomes. The ability of the coordinator and other staff to help the students, through discussion, to relate these out of school experiences to their studies in school and planning a route to university, begins to help them see how they may achieve it. In addition, they may attend one of the schools described by Curtis *et al* (2008), with the sort of institutional habitus of our two independent schools, and a drip feed process through to attendance at a prestigious university.

So, in summary, these young people begin to see themselves as good at learning, and potential university students. Their reservations about being a first attender begin to be assuaged, and they become aware of the micro-steps to achieving their ambition. A new, dynamic iterative interplay between habitus and environment, on the basis of similar ambitions, takes place with and in the new, networked alternative aspiration peer groups, reinforced by the increasing intensity of activities out of school. In a part of their lives, these young people experience the sort of similarity of aspiration which is routine for their peers in independent schools.

Parental interaction

These young people's parents or carers have also attended some of the events organised for them. There are others developed through other urban interventions, as mentioned, for example Education Action Zones. Through their attendance, parents have begun to want to support their children's higher education ambition and have begun to see how they might do this. Their own worries about finance and other risks associated with going to university have also been allayed to an extent, and they may have begun to see, along with their children, 'the relationships between school, higher education and work as a process' (Ball 2003a:84).

Family and community: other social policy interventions

Although much less targeted at university attendance, a number of other policy interventions have been developed in the early years of the twenty first century which are located more broadly socially, and that may affect the relationship between students' experiences in school and those in family and community in Figure 2. In particular, if conceived appropriately and led locally accordingly, they could establish the absolute continuity between school-based learning and aspirations and all others. For potential aspirants for university, there may be the possibility of creating the social bases for the iterative development of aspirational identity, beyond newly networked peer groups, that is the birthright of middle class students.

These policy interventions most notably include Every Child Matters (see DfES, 2004), originally conceived as a joining of traditionally education- and social services-based children's services in response to the violent death of a child in care in North London, but now embracing, under its five objectives and its section of the DCSF website, a range of activities not specifically related to concerns about such children.

Among the interventions most relevant to current considerations is the development of extended schools and extended services – see the prospectus (DfES, 2005b). These extended services variously include study support, increased play, sport and recreational opportunities, special interest groups, support for parents, including through family learning, 'swift and easy access' to targeted and specialist services (such as speech and language therapy) and parental and community access to schools' facilities and programmes, sometimes by their location in the community itself. These activities were supported by substantial amounts of funding in their development phase. Other related activities include learning outside the classroom (see www.lotc.org.uk) and specific provision for children in public care.

Done well, it is possible to see that the social and cultural transitions between school, family and community, the contexts illustrated in Figure 2, will ease. The assumptions, behaviour and language in each may become closer, in the best traditions of community education, and provide firm roots not only for developing aspirational identities, but community attitudes towards lifelong learning as well.

The limitations of these policy interventions
The fragility of success

At its best, therefore, there can be little doubt that some, maybe many, young people, who have all the above experiences, will get themselves to university. Some young people from working class backgrounds have always done it; more will do so with these opportunities. There will be some movement between social classes over the next generation, as there always has been, and these combined policy interventions provide a newer social mechanism for what may have taken different and chancier forms in the past for the most ambitious.

This is a fragile process, however, even when successful, and the policy interventions rely on many complex variables to succeed. What sustains young people from independent schools is a social structure which minimises risk to the formation of aspirational identity in *all* the social contexts of their lives – they have total immersion. And for them this is broadly about reproducing the circumstances of their families. For young people from working class backgrounds, the Labour Government's policy interventions try to recreate or modify social contexts to underpin the iterative development of (socially) different aspirations, but in a much more limited way.

In school, these working class students will still not experience the mono-aspirational context of the independent school, but peer groups who will not only not share their incipient ambition, but be actively hostile to it, with consequences for friends and social life. They will go home with these peer groups; they will be neighbours. The local settings for social gatherings will not be pre-selected as they almost are for the independent school students, especially when boarding. If the young people chosen through AimHigher wish to continue to socialise with their peers, then the story they tell about themselves will need to be more complicated or fractured than that of their independent school peers, because a simple one may not be well received. In an impoverished community, the tug of earning will remain persuasive. And at home, the positive support from parents will still not have the richness of context of the continuing interchange described by parents in Chapter 2 and 3, because of the newness of these parents to these games. Even in schools serving disadvantaged areas considered 'good' or 'outstanding' by Ofsted, and where extended services have succeeded in raising aspirations, extending aspiration in school into their lives outside has proved difficult (Ofsted, 2009).

So, even for someone with great personal qualities of determination and resilience, such as those of Reay *et al*'s (2009) interviewees, which clearly need to be greater than those of students at independent school, the path to university is vulnerable, whatever social changes in expectation there have been about going there and which jobs now require a degree (see Wolf, 2002). And even at the highest functioning level of these interventions, effectively imagined, managed and executed locally, only a minority of the social contexts of these young people's lives will have been modified. No all-encompassing social structure wraps itself round them. Every social context that does not support the iterative development of aspirational identity including university makes it less likely, puts it at risk.

There is thus still no equality of opportunity between working class young people and their independent school peers. University attendance will be and always remains exceptional. This new stream of en-nobled working class talent will replace the small minority of their predecessors who succeeded. It may be a greater proportion than pre-viously, but the positive accumulation of experiences just described will have occurred to date in a minority of settings and for a minority of young people, who, if they had been born in different circum-stances, would have assumed success from an early age and achieved it. This will influence whether these potential students get to university, and where.

Gaps in policy
Ambitious though the Labour Government has been, and worth sup-porting because of it, the complexity of the policy interventions means that its most developed form, which I have just described, will only be achieved in a minority of highly successful schools, even among those achieving maximum access to the programmes.

There may be the continuing problems with the expectations of students mentioned earlier (Raphael Reed *et al, ibid*), for example. There may be problems with providing the iterative discussion with students in school to reinforce and sustain external experiences and relate them to higher education trajectories. And we know from the national evaluation of Excellence in Cities that this aspect of gifted and talented coordinators' work was the one they themselves felt was most likely to be 'squeezed' (Kendall *et al*, 2005), and this was when funding was high and earmarked.

There may not be the knowledge in school about HE routes (see the quotation from Tamsin in the next Chapter), and there may be difficulties about providing a coherent and progressive experience for intending university students. We know, again from the UWE study (Raphael Reed *et al, ibid*), that schools were accessing different aspects of the AimHigher programme, that is, even when they were neighbours and serving similar communities. AimHigher themselves found that one-off aspirational activities were less successful (2006) without being built into a coherent programme for the young person – just the point about the development of aspirational identity. And why, presumably, Aim-Higher South West have stated their intention to develop a 'learner-centred progression programme' during the 2008-11 funding period (AimHigher south west website). Finally, we know from Curtis *et al* (2008) that it is difficult to find schools serving working class communities which are good at sending students to top universities, and provide the drip feed process.

These are possible weaknesses within the minority of schools that have received the complete combined policy formation. But AimHigher has always been targeted, making the minority even more pronounced, as this interchange with Sally, an AimHigher regional coordinator shows:

> Interviewer: ... I get the impression – if you're in a targeted school – let's say one of the Burlingham schools, where historically a smaller proportion of five A*-C students have gone on to HE, or even post-sixteen, then there's going to be loads around. But there must be a lot of schools who are on the margins of those, in the middle of their (performance) tables ... who may see a bit of taster work but don't have any mentors, for example. Although it's a coherent programme, whether you get it or not really depends on what school you happen to be in...

> Sally: That's true, because it is a targeted programme. We do have limited funds and we've got to target some places. I do recognise that there are some kids from under-represented groups in every school. The reason why we target particular schools is because the school environment is quite im-

portant. If you're a working-class kid at a school with relatively high achievement, that very environment will encourage you...We have to target... because we have limited funding. This enables us to target the worst points.

This has been recognised by the government and it has stated its intention to strengthen aspiration raising routes to university into an entitlement (Cabinet Office, 2009a). This is considered in Chapter 8.

Overall, therefore, these programmes are a welcome, albeit an expen-
sive, targeted intervention. It is easy on this basis to understand, for
new reasons, the pessimistic evaluation in Gorard *et al* (2007) of the
success of widening participation initiatives. The programmes described here are unlikely to make more than marginal changes to social
mobility in one generation, unless they are accompanied by a redraw-
ing of occupational structures due to economic change. This is what the
government believes will happen (again, see Chapter 8). Safe reproduction (in the sense of reliable rather than pain-free) from certain
social backgrounds will remain easier and therefore dominant for a
minority of students, because of who and what they are.

That does not mean we shouldn't go on trying. It just means there is
much more we need to do. The managed model of social reproduction
depends on parental agency for it to work to its maximum effect for
independent school students. For their working class peers, effective
agency needs to be exercised by many adults, not just their parents,
from the Secretary of State downwards, through programme managers,
to the teacher keeping the gateway open.

Better jobs, better money?
In parenthesis to this Chapter, I will briefly discuss how a more pessimistic, though contested, view of wider economic matters may further
affect the achievement of widening participation policies and how
there may be disappointments for some of their beneficiaries.

First, there may be caps on the growth of university education itself for
financial reasons related to public sector deficits. An imposed cap on
places for 2009/10 imposed by the Secretary of State, eased at the last
moment by allowing 10,000 unfunded places in science, technology,
engineering and mathematics (STEM) subjects, led to a record number
of qualified students not achieving a university place.

UK Governments have not been alone in expanding higher education for the past 20 years or so: this has been a global phenomenon (Lauder *et al*, 2006), often on the basis of similarly stated motives in relation to competing in the global economy, or economic development, the first of the two policy narratives considered above (Lauder *et al, ibid*). But this growth may cease altogether during the global recession which commenced in 2008.

Second, there may be disappointment when the increased expectations of university, arising from perceived credential inflation, meet the reality of the 'opportunity trap' as Brown (2006) describes it. That is, the percentage of graduate-level jobs in the economy, though expanding, will be lower than the proportion of young graduates entering the job market. Alison Wolf (2002) estimated that, at that time, 30 per cent of graduates were under-unemployed, that is, had jobs which did not require a first degree. It is more complicated than that of course, and will depend on the subjects studied, the university attended and the location of the labour market. But this too will not be helped by the recession and may not be changed by the eventual recovery which succeeds it.

Third, the nature of the developing global economy and how it affects the UK may not be quite how Gordon Brown paints it in the quotation at the beginning of this Chapter. Earlier assumptions about the UK's role depended on taking the view of the 'magnet economy' (Brown and Lauder, 2006). According to this view, developing economies such as those of India and China would perform more basic, less skilled functions in a global division of labour, such as basic manufacturing, which they could do cheaply. Highly skilled tasks such as strategy, gold plating basic products to meet the taste of the sophisticated western consumer (Sennett, 2006), customer relations and finance would be undertaken in Europe and North America. Hence the drive in the UK, because of our skills gap, and elsewhere, to increase skill levels, and specifically the reliance in the UK on financial services to drive the economy, which produced nearly a quarter of UK GDP before the late noughties recession.

This is not how it has turned out. Leaving aside the fact there are still jobs at all levels of skill in the UK, although the balance is shifting, China and India show no sign of accepting a purely low skill role in the world economy. The huge output of graduates mentioned in China and India will allow them to take on highly skilled work to an increasing degree and allow them to compete with the West on *price*, just as they have done previously on basic manufacturing. This is a true skills race, and indeed is already happening. So to keep business in the future, UK companies will have to cut their prices. The future for the UK economy may not thus be high skill, high wage, which is the implication of the Gordon Brown quotation. It may be high skill (essential) but low wage, in order to compete. Those young people inveigled into going to university, who were motivated by the potential middle class lifestyle, may very well thus be disappointed over the next twenty years.

So equal access to the better-paid and more strategic jobs (and the power and influence contingent on them), will be as important as ever for social justice. If there is not more equal access, then the social (class) nature of the elite in a global capitalist system will remain much as it is now, populated by ex-students of independent schools and prestigious universities.

6

Getting in to the right university:
what it is to be bright

What we look for is academic excellence. We certainly like to have people who enjoy other things, are good at sport and ... have got their Duke of Edinburgh award, but that would not be the deciding factor. It's of course ... of interest, but we really look for academic excellence ... (but) when I say excellence, I mean their potential, academic potential, that's what we're looking for, because ... it's the key factor, so of course we pay attention to that.
Admissions Tutor, Oxbridge College

Promoting universities to students from working class backgrounds

Perhaps unsurprisingly considering the performativity of the UK policy context since the early 1990s, the major interventions described in Chapter 5 were accompanied by university benchmarks to be achieved for the admission of young people from lower socio-economic backgrounds. In the UK, this meant people from classes 4, 5, 6 and 7 of the National Statistics Socio-economic Classification (NS-SEC), the classification which replaced the previous registrar-general's five class schemes from 2001. The employment descriptors for the four classes include employment with lower responsibilities than intermediate occupations (such as in an office), the self-employed in small organisations, those in lower supervisory and technical occupations, and those in semi-routine and routine ones. There is no exact equivalence between these categories and the older classes, but they are intended statistically to capture broadly skilled and unskilled manual occupations.

There are also benchmarks for recruitment from priority neighbour-hoods, which are those where university recruitment has traditionally been lowest and which have been targeted by AimHigher. Universities have received premium funding from the Higher Education Funding Council for England (HEFCE) for students who come from them. Finally, there are benchmarks in relation to the admission of students from state schools. These do not help with the consideration of neigh-bourhood and social background, but are interesting in connection with the destination of independent school students.

The data for the 2007/8 academic year released by the Higher Educa-tion Statistics Authority (www.hesa.ac.uk) make interesting reading. Generally, new universities (often former polytechnics) were better at recruiting from both priority postcode areas and from lower socio-economic groups. Prestigious universities have been poorer at both, with much variation between and within these groups.

On the first benchmark in relation to the NS-SEC employment back-ground, Cambridge had achieved 11.0 per cent from these working class backgrounds against a benchmark of 18.4 per cent, Bristol 13.9 per cent against 20.1 per cent, and Oxford 10.5 per cent against 17.4 per cent, the worst in the country that year (and the previous one). By con-trast, East London achieved 50.2 per cent against a benchmark of 38.3 per cent, Bath Spa 30.1 per cent against 31.1 and the West of England 28.2 per cent against 33.8 per cent. Warwick was somewhere in the middle and achieved 17.4 per cent against a benchmark of 20.1 per cent. The percentages of students at each of these universities from independent school backgrounds (the inverse of the state school bench-mark) were Cambridge 43.0 per cent, Bristol 38.5 per cent, and Oxford 46.6 per cent, as mentioned at the end of Chapter 4; East London 1.2 per cent, Bath Spa 4.9 per cent, West of England 10.8 per cent, and Warwick 24 per cent.

Benchmarks are intended to indicate desirable movement from one point to another, of course, and not an absolute situation. But these figures, similar overall to those of previous years, demonstrate the stratification by social class of UK higher education, even while all universities are dominated by students from middle class backgrounds. The more prestigious the university, the greater the proportion of independent school students, and the lower the percentage of students from working class backgrounds. The social structure described in Chapters 2-4 works.

Other policy interventions have been directed at the universities themselves. One of the more prominent was the review of admissions policies resulting in the Schwartz Report (DfES, 2005a), whose language and expectations have now entered, like Leitch, the vernacular of university policies, websites and vice chancellors' speeches. There have also been other less-publicised pieces of work on admissions: *Fair Enough?*, for example, published by Universities UK (2003). This was intended to help admissions tutors make better offers of places, that is, to identify better students who were likely to succeed when they got to university, but who may have been overlooked. So this was about efficiency, not necessarily widening participation.

Finally, universities are now also required to produce access policies, containing the scheme of financial support available to students from less well-off backgrounds. These are reviewed by the Office for Fair Access which, however, does not have the remit to order changes, and there has been an apparent developing trend for bursaries and scholarships to be given on the basis of academic, not financial, merit, according to reported research findings (see Attwood, 2008, in THE). This is similar to the former practice of Oxbridge awards given to candidates who did exceptionally well in the entrance exam.

The admissions tutors and staff interviewed for this research, in old universities and new, were without exception conscientious, and felt a personal and moral obligation, not just legal, to help widen the social basis of university admissions. The move towards widening participation, and hence potentially greater social mobility, however, has not always been popular in prestigious universities. The Vice Chancellor of Cambridge University, Professor Alison Richard, made a speech to her fellow university heads in autumn 2008, criticising 'meddling' ministers, and saying that 'promoting social mobility is not our core mission' (as reported in the *Guardian*, 10 September).

The institutional independence being defended by Professor Richard is often expressed in terms of preserving academic excellence, which in her view can only be done if universities have complete discretion to decide who the very best candidates are. But this is also an argument about the perceived legitimacy or otherwise of using state power to coerce independent institutions which are not producing socially desirable outcomes in the view of the government of the day. This is a critical point for making the UK a fairer society, and will be returned to at several points in the following pages.

Taking Professor Richard at her word, however, champions of widening access have rounded on universities when they have appeared not to be selecting the very best candidates when considering good ones from state schools. Gordon Brown, for example, when Chancellor, became very publicly involved in 2000 when a high performing, straight As student from a state school, Laura Spence, failed to attain a place to read medicine at Magdalen College, Oxford. The whole story can be read on Wikipedia at http://en.wikipedia.org/wiki/Laura_Spence_Affair. Laura might have been one of the Sutton Trust's 'missing 3000' (2005) students from state schools who did not get into top universities in their terms (thirteen in the UK according to the Trust), and who were better qualified at A Level than 3000 peers from independent schools who did so.

Whatever the rights and wrongs of such cases, it must be noted that the Schwartz review (DfES, 2005a) only looked at admissions processes, accompanying its plea to be transparent with a statement that the *content* of admissions, what is to be examined and judged whether it is the 'very best', is the proper business of independent universities:

> Fairness does not mean that the Government should choose students. The Steering Group wishes to affirm its belief in the autonomy of institutions over admissions policies and decisions. Moreover, it should be clearly recognised that it is perfectly legitimate for admissions staff to seek out the most academically excellent students. (DfES, 2005a:6)

And *Fair Enough*, though an interesting and progressive piece of work, did not question the basic structure and academic assumptions of the courses to which students were to be admitted. In short, this has left academics in charge of a secret garden, the likes of which teachers in schools would die for after twenty years of centralised reform.

So, within the context of university admissions, what is academic excellence and what does it represent? And are some young people advantaged more than others by its narratives, in the sense of being more likely to get into prestigious universities?

Who are the best people? Does it matter which university they go to?

Some of the economic reasons why potential university attenders may be disappointed were discussed at the end of Chapter 5. But the stratification of higher education by social class and school of origin just referred to is also a stratification of *perceived worth*, despite, again, the formal equivalence of their degrees. Tamsin expressed this as follows:

> ... it is quite clear, like it or not, that the benefit to be gained from having a degree from... certain universities in this country, is different from that to be gained by having a degree from other universities. It may not be how we would want it to be, but it is how it is ... If you have a degree from (a prestigious university) and you have a degree from (a new university) and you're looking at the two side by side, you do not think of them in the same box. Maybe some people do for certain subjects in certain places, but actually I'm afraid that's much more sophisticated than many people who are in a position of hiring and firing are. *Tamsin, educational charity*

The Sutton Trust as a charity primarily concerns itself with promoting access to prestigious universities, and we know how much difference admission to these universities has made in the past to earnings (Power and Whitty, 2008), and to power and influence. Tamsin's comment embodies this strong presumption of personal worth and worthlessness: the hierarchy of universities corresponds to a perceived, sifted hierarchy of people; it is an ontological ordering, much like general ability.

The Head of Sixth Form at Merryweather expressed this clearly in the following quotation. I had put it to him that being an Oxford graduate, for example, made it much more likely, though not certain, that you would have greater access to power, wealth and influence in our society (following Power and Whitty above), and that was why getting in to the right university was important. He said:

> You do say that Oxbridge graduates have a tremendous... more power, or whatever it is, but that's presumably why they got into Oxbridge – because they're the sort of people who have that facility, who have that ability. It's not the fact that they're Oxbridge graduates; it's the fact that they're very bright, hard-working people... That's why they go to Oxbridge and end up in those positions. The fact that they've been to Oxbridge is not the point... do you realise that most of the British Olympic team have been to Millfield? It's not that Millfield has any advantages of getting into the Olympic team, it's just that people who are very good at sport got to Millfield.

93

And Malcolm, the Oxbridge admissions tutor quoted at the beginning of this Chapter, recognises this view as well:

> I mean it's still the case that people um ... people from good universities are perceived by the outside world as being better; it's a shorthand model of education. They don't feel they've been better educated at Oxford: they feel, they feel themselves to be better by getting in in the first place.

So it is primarily the person not the institution, according to this view. The best people get in to the best universities, and these universities are the best because these people go there. This assumption has a normality about it, just as Merryweather considered preparation for Oxbridge as 'further education'. And the students who are the best are largely clearly middle class, as we have seen, with independent schools well-represented among them.

This puts newer, and less prestigious, universities on somewhat of a back foot in terms of saying what they are good for and at. The solution, reflecting many of their historical roles in preparing students to enter professions such as teaching, is to ally admissions criteria about academic performance (the ontological judgment of worth) with the personal notion of professional vocation, and the specific requirements of particular careers. As Dianna, the head of admissions at a new university, says:

> ... we have some straight academic subjects but so many of them are truly linked into professional areas as well, that it has always been recognised that the highest achievers in national qualifications may not necessarily, therefore, be the right people for certain programmes ... (We are) looking as well for these other qualities and skills, which means the person's going to have ... a particular skill set, or set of personal attributes, which means that they're going to go on through the programme and be able to grasp all the different elements, and then hopefully project themselves into whatever career it is they want.

This is not all professions, of course, but it is a wider group than thirty years ago when some professions such as nursing did not require a degree. It is still only possible to become a doctor by attending one of a relatively small number of medical schools hosted predominantly until recently at older, prestigious universities. But this is a new, distinct role for newer universities and will be important for considering the promotion of social mobility in the sense adopted by the UK Government: that is, making it possible for more people to obtain a job of higher status than their parents. This will be discussed further in Chapter 8.

Broadening the social basis of the professions is certainly desirable as, according to an interim report of the Fair Access to the Professions Panel (Cabinet Office, 2009b), they have become more, rather than less, socially exclusive over the past 30 years. Currently, 'professionals (have) typically (grown) up in families with incomes well above the average family's income' (*ibid*:3) and although only '7% of the population attend independent schools up to age 16 (and 20% to age 18)... those who attended independent schools represent over half of many professions' (p9). This will not be surprising if you have read this far.

And broadening the social basis of the professions is also important for social reasons, as many of their members will become leaders in their local communities, as the final report of the panel says (Panel on Fair Access, 2009). But in itself this does not ensure that those *running* the professions for the next generation, the elite if you like, will come from a wider range of backgrounds. The Panel found that, currently, 70 per cent of top barristers attended independent schools and the figure for judges was nearer 80 per cent. So the social mores – and perhaps the views and colour – at this level of the professions will not radically change quickly.

And the view is less positive for changing the social basis of the elite running transnational companies, which wield unprecedented financial, political and social power in the anonymous globalised economy of the twenty first century, with unfettered movement of money and fractured supply lines. In recent work, Brown *et al* (2008) found that transnational corporations' recruitment policies relied on educational background to screen applicants for their future senior roles. Their human resources departments benchmarked universities before considering candidates, and used world rankings such as those produced by Times Higher Education for this purpose. Recruitment is restricted to a specific number of universities, at the top of the hierarchy. Future elites will therefore be graduates from (some) prestigious universities, but by no means all of them, and from nowhere else.

So certainly for now, the university attended does matter for the fundamental power and wealth structures of our society. The Sutton Trust is right to concentrate on broadening the social basis to, in their terms, 'top' universities. These are where you judge you find the best people, after all. At least for now.

University admissions
General considerations
Whatever the social sifting role of universities may be in relation to future educational and occupational trajectories, admissions staff are trying to select the candidates whom they think are best capable of benefiting from the demands of existing courses, on which they are often teachers.

Admissions staff at prestigious universities use a variety of proxy measures for what they seek, most notably A Levels at very high grades (very often three As). But when there are over ten applications for each place on courses at some of them, they cannot use grades to distinguish between candidates, and use additional methods to decide whom to admit. These include the personal statement of about 500 words candidates are asked to write as part of the common university application form in the UK; formal interviews; marked work sent from their school; a variety of additional entrance tests, including specific national ones for medicine, law and others; and written tests sat by candidates when attending for interviews. The University and College Admissions Service (UCAS) website listed eleven additional tests for admissions to university in 2009.

Admissions staff at three universities were interviewed for this book. These included one of the Oxbridges, another university which was a member of the 20-strong Russell Group of research-intensive universities, and a new, post-1992 university. In each of them, I interviewed the head of admissions, an academic from a subject department involved in making decisions, a widening participation officer if they had one, and other staff as appropriate. For example, staff were interviewed in connection with the development of the AimHigher intervention model described in Chapter 5. I also read critically university admissions policies, both general and subject specific, and prospectuses and websites, and examined in detail how the University and College Admissions Service (UCAS) described and presented its processes.

No more will be said about the universities here as it would make it easier to identify them. Although I interviewed in major departments in each of the universities, I became aware through my reading and visits that there were variations across the institutions, particularly in the Oxbridge and Russell Group universities. At the time of interviews, the admissions decisions there were completely devolved to academics, although each had an agreed central framework for decision making which had been compiled with their help. In the new university, the admissions process was more centralised, but nevertheless the actual processes of decision making were devolved to some of the faculties and schools, and varied between them.

One of the differences at the new university was that an academic's decision was sometimes questioned by central admissions staff, based on the university's agreed criteria. Indeed, I was struck by the fact that university admissions had become professionalised: all three universities provided training and handbooks of various sorts for all staff involved, both academic and administrative.

Another difference was that the admissions task at the Oxbridge and Russell Group universities was to differentiate between candidates and restrict recruitment because of heavy oversubscription. At the new university, courses were not always oversubscribed, though many were, and admissions staff actively sought to offer candidates places, as their head of admissions put it. If candidates met the admissions criteria for some courses, then they would often be offered a place straight away, often as a requirement for courses linked to particular professions.

The new university also allowed extra UCAS points (most post-16 courses and qualifications have such a tariff of points) for students who had taken particular preparation programmes before applying, such as Access Diplomas, or passport schemes. This enabled them to meet the minimum entry requirements more easily. This again made the admissions task significantly different.

One other difference was that the new university, although it had a national catchment for many of its prestigious courses, and had state of the art student residential blocks, was reportedly seen as the local university by many potential students. This enabled it to be more successful in widening participation than its two neighbouring Russell Group universities.

In practice, this makes for quite different sorts of admissions processes across the university sector. But the critical difference, highlighted in the quotation from Dianna, was the supplementing of academic criteria at the new university with a requirement to show understanding of the professions to which candidates were seeking entry, and demonstrate interest in children, the elderly, or disease. To help with this, the university issued a biographical questionnaire as part of its admissions process to some courses. In the Russell Group universities, the most important criteria were academic. I did not interview any Law or Medicine academics in the Oxbridge and Russell Group Universities, however, and so I do not know if personal attributes are as important for these courses. I suspect they are, but even so, they would not override the academic requirements.

Finally, all the staff I interviewed were well aware of the general need to raise aspirations, and specifically, as I have said, to widen the social basis of university admissions. And it was clear from the interviews that the questions sent to them in advance reflected their everyday professional concerns. All interviewees were conscientious and anxious to ensure their respective admissions processes were fair. And for each of them, including academics who had teaching and research responsibilities, the admissions process took a considerable amount of their time during the academic year, not always formally recognised in workloads.

What the universities say they want

The increased transparency in admissions urged by Schwartz has encouraged the setting out on the web of entry requirements for UK university courses, in addition to the traditional paper publications. The following information is taken from reading prospectuses and a series of web searches undertaken between November 2008 and January 2009.

The Oxbridge University sets out its general requirements and information about its selection processes on the web. Tutors, it says, will use GCSE grades as one of the indicators of academic ability, as most candidates will not have taken A Levels when applying, but they will also consider other academic achievements, the personal statements referred to, references and the results of any required written test. The website points out that any conditional offer made (ie dependent on achieving examination success at school) is most likely to be three As. The university is more interested in overall academic ability, however, and candidates' potential and motivation for the course, even if this is different from the courses followed at school.

At the subject level, the university states that tutors will be interested in whether candidates can think clearly and analytically, and less what they know than how they think about and use it. In this humanities subject, tutors will try to discover social and political concerns and candidates' ability to discuss them critically.

Finally, one of the colleges (applications to Oxbridge are made on the basis of subject plus college) states that the most important thing they are looking for is high academic potential. As they say, this is an 'intelligent, enthusiastic and independent-minded interest' in the subject and a willingness to work hard.

At the Russell Group university, general policies and departmental admissions criteria are set out in some detail on the web and in the prospectus, no doubt because they do not interview all potential candidates due to the level of oversubscription. This university tries hard to demonstrate its commitment to be fair, mentioning the training given to interviewers. It describes the range of information taken into account in offering a place, including the recent general performance of the candidate's school or college and 'personal challenges' faced by the candidate.

Nevertheless, here too admissions staff are looking for the 'skills and capabilities' to pursue a degree programme, whether candidates are interested and committed to the subject, can show they have a capacity for critical analysis, clear thinking and expression, including orally, and are able to work independently. Here too, GCSEs are taken into account, but offers will typically be, again, three As or two As and a B. They will, however, consider candidates with an A and two Bs. This university also sets great store on the personal statement, and will look for evidence of 'coherent, analytical and critical thinking' and well-constructed and accurately expressed arguments. The reference from candidates' schools or colleges should provide evidence of their motivation and their 'intellectual inquisitiveness'.

In the new university, I interviewed in a vocational department, whose courses are not directly comparable to those in the departments at the Oxbridge and Russell Group universities, as the degree is also a qualification to practice. Nevertheless, in departmental pages heavy with enticing descriptions of the vocational area, and an outline of the teaching and learning programme, it outlines a typical offer for its courses. This includes five GCSE subjects at grade C and above, including Maths, English Language and Science, and an overall tariff range of 200-240 UCAS points, roughly equivalent to three grade Cs at A Level, but to include specific subjects such as Biology, Science or Social Science.

Access Diplomas were also welcomed at the new university, as has been said, because of the mature entry to many places on courses there. But candidates were expected to demonstrate recent academic study (within the last three years), while being able to put forward significant life and/or work experience for consideration if they did not meet minimum academic requirements. The prospectus makes clear that the university is looking for candidates who are committed to the vocational area, and that they should use the personal statement part of the UCAS form to say why they wish to study it, setting out relevant work experience.

So, although the style is quite different at the new university, successful candidates are expected to achieve the equivalent of just three grades lower over three A Levels than those applying to the Oxbridge and Russell Group universities. These are high achieving students too.

How admissions staff describe their work
All staff interviewed – academic and administrative – referred to their institutions' admissions policies and procedures as the basis for their decision making. What the interviews added to the formally described entry criteria was some insight into how they were applied and how often difficult decisions were made. These comments should therefore

be considered alongside the advertised criteria, and will be discussed together shortly.

The admissions tutors from the Oxbridge and the Russell Group universities gave similar responses to a number of questions. First, Terry on the academic capability they were seeking out. He is referring here to evidence sought from a number of places, including teacher references and the personal statement, as well as the interviews offered to some candidates. These comments are taken from various parts of the interview, in response to different questions:

> ... we're looking for potential, with a sense that potential may not have yet been fully realised in terms of GCSE or AS or A2 grades. And so we take grades into account, but we're probably much more focused on what the teacher is saying about the student and what the student is saying about themselves ... (This) is the most important part of (the application form).

> ... we are looking for enthusiasm about the subject, commitment to the subject, reading wider than just the A-level texts. So there are certain things that are useful to try and latch onto...

> And it's trying to in some way get a sense of whether the student is committed to study, has got some ideas and a spark of something called potential that we could work with. Our interviews are trying to provoke and discover that and ask questions that enable us to get a glimpse of that...

And again:

> ... (we're trying) to discover hidden potential there: is there a sense of trajectory within their exam results. Is that something that teachers are recognising and talking about?

> ... what we're looking for is probably a student who's getting decent A-level results has commitment, (and) has developed independent learning.

A quotation from Malcolm, the Oxbridge Admissions Tutor, heads up this Chapter. As well as being responsible for admissions overall at his particular college, he shares responsibility across the university for admissions to his subject. A much wider group of candidates are given interviews at this university, and so many of Malcolm's answers are related to their conduct:

> ... all the time what one looks for is ... in a general sense, academic potential... (the ability to) present your own views and listen, and take on board,

and critically assess, not just swallow ... (To) critically assess any point of view (that one) might produce. So that's the sort of thing...

And in terms of how candidates present:

... it doesn't matter at all if they're at ease or quick witted, we want someone who ... has his or her own ideas, is prepared to listen to alternative ideas, and is prepared and able to synthesize and make something out of them. That's what ... my ideal candidate would be.

For Malcolm, the interview responses from candidates can also be a good measure of how they will be able to benefit from the style of teaching in Oxbridge, through small group or individual tutorials. The two go hand in hand for him. So he will see:

... what sort of things interest (them). (I'll) pick a topic or two and see what they make of them, see if they can synthesise and get beyond that.

On the other hand:

... it's a bad sign if they say 'no, no, it can't be, it just can't be'. What you want is for them to put an alternative view, or say 'well, I don't quite understand the point about that', or 'I can see how that addresses one part of problem but not the other half', or something like that. So, that's one of the things we look for...

And after a discussion of apocryphal stories about Oxbridge interviews (such as being asked to define a paper clip!), he said:

... often I will say, 'take your time'. Some of the candidates feel ... it's like a chat show and they must be quick at repartee. And often I would much prefer someone who says 'give me a minute, I'm not quite sure', who actually thinks rather than just comes out with a quick clever response ... I think (we) would prefer something thoughtful rather than something quick. It's not that we don't allow them to think that fast. It's just that some people think quickly, but it's not in itself the criterion...

As well as the academic potential, therefore, Malcolm emphasised that they were also clearly looking for 'teachability', the 'ability to benefit from a tutorial, from tutorial style teaching'. He gave an example from one of his current students who described his own admissions interview as a 'mini tute'.

For Terry, this was also important, but not always so integral to the selection process, as not all candidates offered places would have been interviewed. Nevertheless, he said that:

> We need to get a sense of whether this student could cope as a first year student – and although there are possibilities for them to develop skills and for us to try and do as much as we can – we have to have someone in the position where they're starting to think like a first year undergraduate.

Admissions tutors, according to Terry, must ask 'could this student cope: would this student benefit and be the kind of person that would really thrive as an undergraduate?'.

By contrast, the key criteria for Veronica, the admissions tutor at the new university, after meeting minimum entry criteria, was ensuring candidates were aware of the nature of the profession they should be entering in three years' time, and whether they were likely to be able to meet its demands:

> ... what we are looking for is insight into the profession... gained either by visiting a department, talking to professionals that work in the area, talking to (people who) ... have used the service, friends, neighbours, or attending open days. We say that that experience can be gained in a broad way, so we are not totally prescriptive that you must do this.

Nevertheless, she was critical of the ways in which some candidates had not taken these steps before being asked to be considered for a place on the course.

Getting the right candidates

The selection task is therefore matching what the candidate has the potential to be and the demands made by the current structure of the undergraduate course, without really examining what those demands are or whether they should be different. This is understandable for a course linked to a nationally governed profession, but perhaps less so for academic degree courses where eligibility is being assessed as above. The *Fair Enough?* study already referred to (Universities UK, 2003) fitted in to this operational context.

There is an obvious danger related to this, that admissions tutors, who may be teaching the candidates next academic year, may pick people like them, or at least, people who were like the people they have enjoyed teaching. Terry was well aware of this:

> ...if you pick the students you know you'll be teaching next year ... are you choosing students bearing similarities to certain students you've taught in the past?... It's a critical issue for admissions tutors to reflect on.

As was Veronica:

> ...all the research has shown that we actually favour people that are like our-selves, so that's always going to be a danger...

Awareness does not mean that this is no longer a problem. Although potential is being sought, and not the fully-fashioned and formed first year undergraduate, a theme of nearly all the interviews was that there was only so much universities could do by the time it came to the admissions process. Terry again:

> We have to try and get the very best students, but we're also realistic about the fact that they need to be some way along in an educational process, meaning they're not going to come in at zero, but they're going to need to come in at eight.

He means in the sense of ten out of ten being fully ready to perform as an undergraduate. The problem was what had happened to them at school. So recognising what the candidates may become, given how they are now, becomes the crucial issue.

All staff interviewed were aware of weaknesses in the interview process as a means of judging the suitability of candidates. One was the need to ensure candidates did not feel intimidated and were able to represent themselves adequately:

> ... we try and work with what they offer and have a series of questions that take that deeper. We start in a very surface way with the thing they're im-mediately doing ... but try and get a sense of what else is going on. Not push them in a confrontational way, but encourage deeper reflection from the stu-dent. *Terry, on interviewing access students*

> ... we want to find out about the person we're interviewing ... We make them feel at ease, let them talk about things that interest them, let them show the very best of themselves. There's no point whatsoever in us trying to wrong foot them, trip them up, this sort of thing. (But) ...good candidates we will cer-tainly press. *Malcolm*

And Malcolm also described the process whereby candidates called for interview were in residence at his college for a few days, and so could begin to feel more at home. But he was very candid about the extent of preparation that had occurred by the time it came to interview:

> We do try to see if we can see through it, because we can't say that even if we get a polished candidate, we ... can always successfully tell what's polish and what's not. But we are well aware of the problem and we do everything we can to allow for that...

But sometimes they do see through it:

> I won't mention the schools, but there are some very well known public schools ... (which) send us people (who) have been on paper extraordinarily good people, but ten minutes into interview you realise that ... (they're) not going to make it...

On the other hand:

> ... (some) people who come pretty close to the borderline (for being called for interview) ... do impress us very much. So there is indeed a lot to be learned from that.

And Veronica, although she is required to interview, felt as follows:

> I personally don't see a lot of point in interviewing, ...because there are people I have interviewed that make the course that are absolutely horrendous when they get here. They've been coached. (The interview) ...is entirely coachable.

The degree of polish, or coaching, was a common refrain in the interviews: candidates are coached to perform as potential undergraduate students from the earliest stages. Dianna, head of admissions at the new university, recognised this when talking about the possibility of going back to the candidates for further information if needed after receipt of the UCAS form:

> We do sometimes go back to the applicants, although they are now so well schooled and drilled, that in most cases you have all the information you require on the form.

The coaching and drilling begins with filling in the form, which means the personal statement is considered drilled also, but not equally or effectively from all schools and colleges. Veronica, at the new university, is talking about access students in particular here:

> ... but there's a problem with supporting statements in that they are often heavily coached in my opinion, particular those from access courses... where ... they receive the credit for submitting the UCAS form with a specially constructed supporting statement. So if that's been seen and corrected by the

105

staff within the FE college, it may have been corrected four or five times and I can tell now which college some of them are at by reading the supporting statement. Because they've been coached to do it in a certain way... a lot of the supporting statement I'm afraid I consider meaningless.

Consider also the drip feed process in Chapter 3 and the amount of time spent at the independent schools on writing and rewriting the personal statement. This is the principal means whereby some students are considered in the department at the Russell Group university; the task for the student and his or her advisers is to craft the statement to meet the openly advertised criteria. So this has become another game.

But Cambridge, apparently, who interview routinely for admission, have decided not to assign marks to the personal statement, precisely because of not being able to tell who wrote it (reported in the *Guardian* 19 May, 2009).

The variable degree of coaching is also seen in the two pieces of written work submitted for consideration at the Oxbridge college. Malcolm here speaks of his experience:

... likewise written work. Well, different people interpret it in different ways. It has to be said that some schools help people with their written work rather more than others ... There's the possibility of straight plagiarism and lifting the thing straight off the web. But there's also the possibility that in some schools the teacher might say 'here's a good topic to write on ... here are some good thoughts and you might want to say the following'. And after they've done it, they might say 'you might want to rewrite it...' On the other hand, in some schools they might say 'if you want to write something, it's up to you'.

The degree of student preparation does vary, as was discussed in the last Chapter. Terry described the intention behind the Russell Group university's being open and transparent (as Schwartz recommends): it is to try and avoid giving advantages to the products of some schools rather than others:

... the idea is that rather than admissions being this kind of secret that maybe certain people have access to, and in particular if your school has a full-time careers/UCAS officer who can speak to admission tutors and get access to information about the types of things we're looking for, our sense is to actually make that entirely transparent.

The description of the 'full-time careers/UCAS officer' or equivalent role may be, again, familiar from Chapter 3. But even if Terry and Malcolm and their colleagues manage to see the true potential of candidates through their various admissions processes, both their universities have limited room for manoeuvre in making different grade offers.

Terry explains how they will make the conditional offer, taking into account the educational context of the school, after consideration of the personal statement:

> Our admission strategy is to attract the very best students from their school, but our sense is that the very best student from a school where the average A-level score is a hundred and twenty points may have different grades from a student where the average score is four hundred points. And we need to recognise that, and understand that students are coming from an educational context ... That's where we've tried to read the form within a bigger context of the kinds of information we now get from UCAS about schools, and in particular the kinds of average A-level points as an indicator of whether this student is above average, average or below average really.

This is where, as described earlier, the teachers' comments are taken into account and Terry and his colleagues try to see if there is 'any sense of trajectory', in which case they may make an offer conditional on lower grades.

The context, however, is also the 'level of competition' as Celia, the head of admissions at this Russell Group university, said:

> ... the main reason that applicants are unsuccessful (here) is because of the level of the competition. I know it varies a lot between courses but overall we have eleven applicants per place, so a lot of applicants, well over 50% of all our applicants, whatever school they come from, are going to be unsuccessful.

And the vast majority of these applicants will have high predicted grades, making differentiation difficult. At Oxbridge, Malcolm was discussing the standard AAA offer outlined earlier:

> When we say three As, we had someone, let's see, with seven As, so we do tend to see (a narrow range of results) ... If they were sort of distinguished between A1, A2 and A3, or something, then in that case we might well say three A1s for someone from Eton and three A3s for someone from some

other school. But it's more difficult given that they make such a broad scatter of it now ... (but) we would be entirely happy (with that). What we're trying to do is to look at potential. I think we would be entirely happy with it in principle.

So although tutors here also look at the contexts of applicants' schools, including GCSE results, in practice, as the then acting head of admissions at the Oxbridge university said:

... the one clear thing that does not happen is that there is a reduction in offer... You know 99% of our students get two As and a B or more, and something in the 90%s of students get three As, so we don't (change) ... our offer. I think that's quite clear.

Commentary and summary

I am going to concentrate for a few paragraphs on Oxbridge and the other Russell Group University. It is not the case that admissions to the new university are unimportant, or that new universities in general do not offer opportunities to young and older people to learn, acquire skills and get a better job than their parents. They do (see million +, 2009), and, subject to the reservations to be expressed in Chapters 5 and 8, in so doing they enable some degree of social mobility.

But the Oxbridge and the Russell Group university are prestigious universities, in the sense of usually appearing in the top ten UK universities in the various league tables produced by the *Guardian, Times* and so on (see Attwood, 2009). They are therefore important for the recruitment of elites and historically for disproportionate access to power, wealth and influence. And ex-independent school students are over-represented in them.

All this has been said. What will be explored for the next few pages, however, is an unanticipated outcome from these data, namely that the social structure which works so well for independent school students appears also to be underpinned by *words*. Indeed, it will be argued, words are an important part of the fabric of this social structure: there a remarkable similarity between the descriptions of academic potential just examined and parents' descriptions of their children while at the two independent schools.

For ease of reference, I will summarise what these two prestigious universities are looking for in terms of academic potential, a composite of what was described by tutors and the universities' various paper and electronic publications. The sample is of course small – it is only a snapshot – and a much larger one would be needed to confirm the descriptions here, but the similarities between these two universities, across all the staff interviewed in each, suggest that similar descriptions will be found elsewhere. A social process seems to have been alighted upon here.

So the academic potential sought by the two universities needs to be almost formed, and include the capability of thriving as a first year undergraduate. Tutors seek interest in, enthusiasm for, and commitment to the subject in potential students. Students will have read round the subject and beyond the A Level texts. Although not needing to be *fast* thinkers, they need to be clear and analytical. They will listen carefully to, and assess critically, evidence, arguments and views put to them. They will synthesise information and different viewpoints, and be able to present their own views coherently and constructively. What they know now is not as important as how they think about, use and express it. Potential students are expected to be inquisitive and motivated and able to work independently.

But bear in mind that all the staff interviewed had reservations about all the means of assessing these qualities, not least because of the variable degrees of coaching and preparation which have taken place. And even though all interviewees were keen to widen access, they also made it clear that the students should be almost ready to be undergraduate students by the time of application. Further, though they either made differential grade offers or would like to, related to the performance of applicants' schools or colleges, there was limited scope for this because of the quality of the applicants overall. In any case, at the Russell Group university, there had to be some sense of a trajectory.

One other reservation: the two university subjects considered here were in the humanities, and so any of the nine additional tests, such as those for medicine and law, were not being employed. It is beyond the scope of this book to comment on the reliability of these tests, but of course it is also the case that in some schools, such as Merryweather, potential students were prepared routinely for them, whereas in others there was little experience of their students needing to take them at all.

Parental statements of entitlement

Parents made a variety of qualitative statements about their children when asked to introduce their family, incidentally in response to other questions, and in describing their reasons for going independent, which, it has been argued, should not be recognised as a choice of school but rather a choice of social trajectory. Similarly, it will be argued here that these descriptions can also be regarded as statements of entitlement.

Some of the tension implicit in parental descriptions, requiring the pro-activity discussed, was between their perceptions of their children's attributes and capabilities on the one hand, and their recognition and fulfilment through chosen schools and trajectories on the other. Comments made in the interviews were often based on obvious achievements, but also on a developed sense of pecking order. We have already seen Charlotte, a Merryweather parent, saying that her son regarded himself as a 'rung below Oxbridge' (Chapter 2, p19), but she went on to describe various 'courses and interviews' he went on, including a 'really demanding' one for 'leadership', after which he nevertheless achieved a Sandhurst scholarship.

Ann, a Carter's parent, described her daughter as 'one of those where all her friends ring her up for advice on how to do their Maths'. And Deborah, with children also currently or previously at Carter's, described three of her children thus:

> A great sportsman, intellectually he's quite bright, not perhaps as bright as (his brother) but he got a fist full of A-Cs in GCSE and A, B, C in his A-levels ... he mixed sciences and arts at A-level ... and he used to play county sports as well. He used to play county hockey and cricket. So he was [a] good all rounder ... he's a bright kid, he's no mug and he's immensely talented as far as sport and art is concerned.

> He's read a phenomenal amount and he's a kid that reads *The Times* from cover to cover every morning. ... He's very aware and alert, so I think 'well, good luck to you sunshine' because ... his ambition is to be a film producer ... and he's been very sure from a very early age of what he wants to do... He's a very musical boy, taught himself to play the guitar... I think he will be very successful in what he wants to do ... but also, you know, he's an intellectual as well.

I suspect she will get a run of As to Cs ... I would say, she's a good average, slightly above average intellect ... I think she will be successful, she's quite single minded, she's very self contained as a person ... She's hugely popular socially. She is befriended by sixth form boys and girls alike and kids lower down in the school.

Fay, with children at Merryweather and other schools, describes her son and daughter thus:

He did get ten A stars. He has got very high AS Levels, very high: out of 300, over 295. (He) is ... good across the board. The Classics master wanting him to do Classics at Oxford, the languages people, you know ... he was right across the board and ... (And) he was top of the year in history.

My daughter, who's doing her GCSEs, is very much artistic and musical. She ought to be [a] human rights lawyer, but she really enjoys philosophy and ethics and stuff, and so I think she will do a degree in that first, and see where that leads her...

Jenny, Carter's, describes the acquisition of literacy by her daughter before starting school. She is now a medical student:

She started reading very early of her own accord ... She would ask me what she saw was written ... And she understood. (We) do lots of things at home (but) I didn't push her ... She was quite receptive ... she was very into the written word.

Kerry made a number of reflective comments about her son who is in the sixth form at Merryweather:

He was obviously very bright, and it hadn't occurred to me ... He's an academic child, he enjoys studying ... He's always been interested in history and classics right from the start – it's always been his favourite subject ... He was going to look for dinosaurs like most little boys, but he's moved more into archaeology and studying history ... and he loves languages ... I think that he obviously has a flair for learning the languages.

He has always been interested in words. Right from being very small, he's always read a lot and he was always trying to write before he really even could. He would dictate things to me and I would have to write (them down).

He's thought about journalism as well – he has a love of writing, so I think that would appeal ... (He's) always been the sort of lad who ... takes a lot of time to mull things over. He processes them on his own.

It ought to be said that Kerry's very positive comments were also interspersed with apparently realistic notions of her son's limitations. Two last comments:

> ... (and) he has a particular gift for picking up how people speak. He listens and it's not lost on him – he's almost a photographic memory. He's good at dialects and regional variations. He's doing German, French, and he did Italian GCSE this year, just to do another language, because he had the chance ... And in every other respect he's a bright, intelligent, attractive, gifted and able young man. And he's hard working. *Peter, on one of his sons at Merryweather*

> (He's) very awkward and argumentative. He always has to be right. And I think he usually is right, which is more annoying. But ... a born leader. When he was at school, he would be captain ... he wasn't one year, but he had a bad leg then.

> All he wanted to be ... was basically to earn lots of money. That's all he wanted. He's a snappy dresser, he likes clothes, he likes cars, he wants to buy a Porsche ... In his GCSEs he got ten As, six A*s and he got 3 A-levels – As – and he was chosen to do a special paper you have to be asked to do, and he got top marks in that. But because of how he is... I mean, he's a sportsperson, because he's a woman's man, he's an academic, and he's really an all-round person, you know ... *Adrian, talking about the elder of his two sons who had gone to Merryweather*

These comments have by no means exhausted the data. Among other stories, a boy was 'astounded' he had only been awarded an A, rather than an A* in his exam. And in another case, a boy had written his SATs answers at primary school back to front, in mirror writing. But, nevertheless, they were all correct!

These stories were often related with a sense of pride and achievement, but not overweeningly so: this was normal for them. Many of the parents were too clear of the risks to their children's trajectory, though objectively they were secure. Nevertheless, as a group, they are structured as statements of entitlement: because my child is like this and has these qualities, they are entitled to attend a school of a certain sort which makes particular provision for them. Among these parents, the sense of entitlement had been realised by choosing and gaining access to an independent school, often, it must be said, against the perceived poor quality on offer at state primary and secondary schools, but not always.

Here are some of the examples of this:

He's one of these children that need to be pushed. He was just not being pushed at that school at all, which was when we came and had a look at the lower school here, liked what we saw and decided we'd move him there.

... one of the drivers for moving her was because at Bolingbroke (state primary), they had this situation whereby they would have two years in the same class, and where you've got bright children that is fine if they're the lower group in a multi-tiered class. But once they're the top group, you don't get the challenge. *Ann, Carter's*

I'm not a competitive parent but I think he ought to be in the top stream. Nobody would have it. And he would do extraordinarily well in exams ... and then when he came to decide, they'd put him down to do dual award science ... (And) I was cross because ... he's smart. And the proof was in the pudding because, hello, he got three A*s. But I felt the staff were reluctant actually to listen to me and it took quite a while to say 'look....', you know... *Deborah, Carter's*

(He) didn't enjoy primary school at all: he did the first year in a state school and at the end of that they called us in and said ... they couldn't cater for him, that they had gone through the books for the school ... and ... their education authority ... couldn't provide the resources they felt necessary for him at the age of five. Well he was five and a half or whatever, he had just done the reception year. *Fay, Merryweather*

But as Fay said in Chapter 4 (p43), her son fitted in well at Merryweather, in a 'niche ... of similar boys', who were 'all fairly studious and quiet'. Kerry, also with her son at Merryweather, relates similar things in this interchange:

Kerry: He had been marked down as special needs at primary school and there weren't the resources to help him.

Interviewer: In terms of gifted and talented?

Kerry: Yes. The teachers were wonderful but they didn't have the resources. I mean he was obviously above the standard of the other children, so I felt he needed an extra push and extra help to keep his interest going.

Interviewer: You didn't think you'd find that in the local state school?

Kerry: No, I didn't. We looked round all the schools and thought about it very carefully.

And the comment here, reproduced from Chapter 4 in full, for its significance and ease of reference:

> The things that he was reading ... we looked around and at some schools I thought 'well no, Jo's well beyond this already', so he did need an extra push. It's having other kids who're on the same level as him to discuss books and things ... he had brilliant friends at primary school but they didn't have ... the same sort of interests. So I think that's why he fitted in here, because there were other boys the same as him.

Lynne, with one son at Merryweather and one elsewhere, similarly explains how her son settled in:

> Within this school ... you're inundated with talent and clever, successful, motivated children ... One of the things that makes it unique is that the cleverer you are, it's not a problem, whereas in state schools you can be almost hounded for being that way... There are lots of weird and wonderful kids here, and my (son) doesn't really fit in that weird and wonderful bracket, but he's absolutely running with them. My godson ... lovely boy, but he's on a different planet. They don't mind, and no one's never saying, 'why did you do that?'

Finally Peter said 'we looked at the local provision and we were terrified' (showing how 'unthinkable' some options are for middle class parents – Ball, 2003a:65). But once at Merryweather:

> ...we thought it was good because they were thinking laterally, they were free thinkers. And when we looked round the school, we saw one boy going past down the corridor, juggling!

> But I'll tell you what they don't do: they don't recognise mediocrity. You know, you don't get a certificate for being there. That's a difference I've noticed from primary to secondary, but also in this school, they don't say 'well done' if it's just ordinary. There's not much that's ordinary around here, do you know what I mean?... I can't remember what they said, but it was something like 'excellence is normal here'.

Commentary and summary

Thus a composite set of parentally composed characteristics of these young people, might read as follows.

These young people are able, bright or very bright, intelligent, ahead of their peers at primary school, academic, gifted and talented, intellectual, and with leadership potential. They are all-rounders, sporty, and socially successful. They read a lot, phenomenally, *The Times* from cover to cover. They love words and writing. They listen well and may have a gift for picking up how people speak. They have developed early interests in particular academic subjects (archaeology, history, philosophy, classics, languages) or careers (human rights lawyer, journalist).

The parents' sense of entitlement arises from their children's need to be pushed, challenged, be in the top stream, have access to a wider range of books and resources than those available in primary school. They need routinely to be with other children like them, who may be talented, clever, motivated, possibly weird and wonderful, are on the same level to discuss books 'and things', and are free and lateral thinkers.

For these parents, their sense of entitlement has been realised or enhanced by places at independent schools, but often began with state schools not being able to cater for their children, in their view, and their not having either the appropriate resources or peer group.

The validity of these data: my (unrecognised) bright child

The parents were selected for interviews by their children's schools, and may have exaggerated their own proactivity. But this was allowed for in considering proactivity as a critical ingredient for getting the most out of the managed model of social reproduction (Chapter 4). The model will still work without it, however, and the level of proactivity is nothing like that required at all levels of the system to make the policy interventions work described in Chapter 5.

But it was the informality and the similarity of these comments that suggested they may have wider currency, both in terms of describing children's talents and the notion of achieving recognition of them from schools and teachers. That they do has been suggested by the ESRC study already mentioned (James and Beedell, 2009; Crozier *et al*, 2008) and Lucey and Reay (2002) highlight 'the unquestioned belief that middle-class parents have that their children are clever, or at the very least, have great potential', such that they need 'levels of input which they perceive are not available in the local ... comprehensive schools' (p329).

And their wider currency was confirmed by surveying a variety of websites over 2008 and 2009. Included were websites where parents can discuss problems with peers – a sort of electronic school gate – or seek advice from experts. Evidence came from live threads on:

www.education.com; www.ukfamily.co.uk
www.ukparentslounge.com; www.practicalparenting.co.uk;
www. raisingkids.co.uk; www.mumsnet.com; www.netmums.com;
www. mychild.co.uk; www.parents.org; www.parents.co.uk;
www.bright starters.co.uk; www.parentsconnect.com.

But I also drew on sites where just advice for parents and professionals was posted, without necessarily any facility for discussion or response. These included the UK Government's www.parentscentre.gov.uk site, those of councils (for example, a London Borough website included *suggestions for parents of able children*), MENSA, the National Association for Gifted Children and some national newspapers. These latter sometimes carry a thread of online comment after a particular opinion piece.

An immense number of topics are covered on these combined websites, and range from pre-natal to applying for university. Many stories are told about children, but the entitlement narratives of brightness, and the difficulty, just as for the parents interviewed for this book, of getting what parents want or need out of school, are there in a good proportion of entries. As are the notions of unrecognised and unrewarded ability – the identification issue for gifted and talented discussed in Chapter 5.

The following brief extracts are taken from themes, titles, discussion topics and contributions. They are grouped and broken up at some points to make them intelligible out of the web context. These particular ones are all made by different people.

> Bright child, low average attainment 'cos specific learning diffs, role of school? ... My 15 year old daughter still cannot spell or punctuate ... She is predicted A/A* for content ...

> Good luck everyone who is not happy with the way your child's school is handling things and I hope you all find the help and support you need....

> I know exactly what you mean about being unsure what to push for – I get easily put off when teachers act dismissive ... Since I made loads of fuss a few weeks ago... my daughter loves writing

Like yours, my (daughter) is really bright – certainly in the way she thinks and talks – but finds it really hard to learn at school ...

This type of child is hardest to get help for ... Exactly because they are bright with lots of potential ...

... school aren't bothered ...

Too bright for teacher? ... My 6 year old is very alert to her surroundings... when the Mir space station was coming down, she watched it intently on tv ... she began excitedly to tell her teacher about it... (but) the teacher just shrugged ... (*Reply from expert*): You certainly have a bright little girl there!

My bright 16 yr-old is on the verge of dropping out of college just three months into his AS-levels ... (*Reply*) You say your son is bright, and if he could get A or B grades without too much catching up, he certainly is...

(*Another expert reply*): ... try to determine whether it's a case of ability or confidence ... often the performance of people with ability does not live up to expectation ... due to factors such as ill health, emotional upsets or even practical issues.

How can I help my very bright child develop social skills? ... (*Reply*) the socio-emotional development of a gifted child can be very difficult...

Intelligence (is) not enough to succeed in school ... my son is bright, above average in many ways ... more than a 100-watt bulb in a galley of dim candles ... (but) you'd never tell from his (school) grades ... (which are) in at least the top 10 per cent ... on a standardised scale...

My little boy is currently in year 1... he has always been a very bright boy – he knew the alphabet at 14 months and was reading fluently by $2\frac{1}{2}$ years ... He had various problems in pre-school ... being disruptive due to being bored...

Anyone else out there who has a Gifted and Talented child? ... (Mine) is 5 and a half and we knew she was special since she was ... 1 year old. By 16 months she could read all the letters of the alphabet which she learnt by herself... She was a fluent reader before she was 3 ... she has a really strong memory, more for visual and factual things ...

... at the moment we have a problem with my eldest (still only 5) in that she has 'given up'. It is all boring and she won't do stuff ...

My son is only $2\frac{1}{2}$ ... he's definitely quite far ahead of his peers... He's been able to recognise the alphabet for quite a while ... Now he has a large vocabulary ... he's just started wanting to form letters ... Hubs has a 150s IQ ... so all this leads me to think Son is going to be quite bright ...

> My son has been moved into a mixed age class... the older kids are bored, the teacher has no support and does not seem to be coping ... From being a bright happy social child I have an unhappy lonely child who is falling behind ... I have complained ...

> I have a longstanding concern that she will be bored and or not challenged enough at school ... My big fear is that ... at school ... she will languish, play, muck about, get bored until all the other children 'catch up', and by then she will have lost the impetus to learn...

> When I briefly spoke to her teacher... she just talked about teaching her phonics, completely missing the point that she already reads superbly ... I had a similar response from my son's teachers, saying that they couldn't let him have books that were above the level of the class until he had been tested ...

These may well be statements of the 'entitled middle class self' (Skeggs, 2004), or not, as we cannot confirm the background of anonymous or pseudonymed correspondents. But the following final quotation should remind all of us who read these entries out of detached interest of the anguish which lies behind some of them:

> I think you sound like a fantastic mum and you should be very proud of all the hard work you do with your son. As mums we never stop worrying...

These chat rooms have all the advantage of raw, revealing immediacy. More removed perhaps are the sentiments expressed in various parenting guides in print, but the same entitlement narratives are there in the ones which include sections on schooling or education more generally. Wilce (2004) and Gilbert (2007), for example, are very much for the Education Consumer – how to make sense of and get the most for your child out of school admissions, how to choose the right school, how to assess it, including the headteacher, how to appeal and how to complain once a place has been secured. And both these books have short sections on giftedness, and talk about the possibility of the gifted child becoming bored if not stretched. Gilbert includes a description of a parent complaining about a child not being put in the top set. These books situate education as a series of important encounters in the realisation of children's life projects.

Wilce also includes a Chapter on 'learning to learn – better' (p157-177) where, among other matters, she explores whether it is worth getting your child's IQ assessed (not necessarily), after explaining CATs. But the notions of entitlement are here, albeit softened. In Tynan (2008), written to accompany a television series, the subtitle of *uncovering your child's hidden gifts* echoes the discussion in Chapter 5. The notion of the book is about how 'brilliant' you and your child are, or will be (Chapter 10), and therefore, again, choosing the school which is right, and getting the most out of it.

In short, the narratives about my bright child, as statements of entitlement, are certainly found much more widely than in the group of parents interviewed. They are common currency in vernacular and visible discussions of parenting and the data presented in this book so far do therefore represent a wider phenomenon.

Transforming narratives of entitlement into academic potential

The starting point for transforming entitlement narratives is that there are some very similar formulations between the two sets of descriptive statements employed by academics and parents:

- The academics' desired interest in, and enthusiasm for, the subject in their potential students, is reflected in the parents' descriptions of early developing interest in a range of academic subjects – archaeology, history, philosophy, classics, languages as above – and wider activities outside (in these cases drama and sport)

- Potential students, according to the academics, need to have read round the subject and beyond the A Level texts. The parents described their children's extensive reading (and writing) habits – often of books well ahead of those provided for their peers

- The academics seek clear and analytical thinking, though not necessarily fast thinkers; potential students will be able to listen carefully to, and assess critically, arguments and views put to them, and be able to present their own views. According to their parents, the independent school students are quick (or bright) and persuasive individuals. They listen well, picking things up quickly and mulling things over

So independent school students are hearing these narratives about themselves in the home, perhaps as part of discussions about career pathways and, through the social processes of developing aspirational identity, are taking on similar self-narratives about themselves. At a deep ontological level, they are beginning to think about themselves in ways which will be appropriate in a university context. This is good preparation for writing a UCAS personal statement and going to interview. The terms they will have acquired in the particular discursive practice within which their self-narratives are being expressed will be the ones that spring to mind, at a deep level from habitus, when writing and being interviewed. This is how social structure works – through the very words we use.

The transformational and preparatory task for these students' independent schools is therefore clear and much more straightforward than that facing schools preparing aspirant working class students for university, whose home narratives may be positive and supportive, but whose parents may not be pursuing 'middle class cultivation techniques' (Gillies, 2007:97). Unless enrolled through one of the policy interventions, the greater distance between home and school narratives may be exacerbated here from an early age by parents' more limited concerns about staying out of trouble, and by contact with school being limited to formal occasions such as parents' evenings (Gillies, *ibid*). In the middle class home, children will continue to be 'presented with possibilities' about themselves in terms of what they are like and capable of, as Lynne, one of the Merryweather parents, said.

So to reach the characteristics of academic potential, the independent school ensures and deepens the academic grounding for university entrance and polishes it up. Both the independent schools visited (and many more on the web) expound the academic qualifications of their staff, including at doctoral level. 'Scholarship' was expressed as a core value at one of the schools visited and both boasted that a measure of good teaching was going beyond the requirements of the syllabus, just as the admissions tutors said. Love of the subject was important. In subject lessons, and through wider complementary studies, students will have learned how to put up an argument and defend themselves. More particularly, meeting alumni like them who have been to prestigious universities, they will learn to project mentally how they will settle into university life with more people like them. 'Should go to university', and what it means, will have become an ontological statement in the context of their schools, to complement those being taken on from home. They will have come to think they are entitled to go and settle at university in general, if not at particular ones.

The closeness of independent schools to prestigious universities is maintained by the continuing links of senior staff, regular speakers to remind pupils about going there, and conferences to enable them to make the link with professional careers, as part of the drip-feed process. Their closeness is even expressed in their buildings – in these cases, ivy-clad and set out round quadrangles. Finally, the drip-feed process will ensure nothing will be left to chance at these, as it happens, mono-focal establishments. Thus, the parental narratives which help lay the constantly iterative foundations for the development of these young people's self view, underpinning their identity, will be polished, converted, deepened and supplemented into the ones sought by universities. Entitlement is then realised.

Social implications
The upshot of the microstudies undertaken for this book and this wider survey of discursive practices of (apparently middle class) parenting appears to be that notions of scholarship, and academic potential, are owned by middle class parents. They are closer to their lives, with the complete and complex cultural congruity between family life, leisure activities and expectations, and the defining expressive and instrumental orders of the classroom, especially in independent schools.

It could be said that this is because middle class parents are generally better at it, as Dave Aaronovitch writes in *The Times*:

> The reason why some children do far better than others is obvious ... One parent in my daughter's class complained that her six year old son ... was in no condition to do the boring reading that the school expected ... Boys play football she announced ... Money itself is rarely the explanation ... Perhaps one reason for the growing advantage of the middle classes is not that they are richer, but just that they assimilate better all the dire warnings about face-time, junk food and smoking. None of it is a mystery... (*June 12th, 2007*)

But the issue is the closeness of everyday narratives – in school, at home and in the community – to that of academic expectation and universities. The existence of these narratives, and the discursive practices within which they are formed, are the social counterpart of the process Cremin and Thomas (2005) describe as 'maintaining the underclasses', in their case, by the use of what they describe as 'contrastive judgment' through 'everyday constructs'. Together, they illustrate that the terms in which young people are described and in which they begin to describe and consider themselves, help maintain social differences from one generation to the next. Appreciating this point is critical to an understanding of social structure.

But although these narratives and experiences may be normal in professional middle class homes, this does not mean they should not become normal in working class ones. This requires major interventions, beyond the scope of current ones. And such interventions *are* interfering with social structure – why should we not? Radnor *et al* (2007), in an article drawing from interviews with school gifted and talented coordinators on how they do their work, including pushing potentially first time university attenders, describe how coordinators try to induct students into middle class thought habits, by:

> ...[focusing] in on those pupils that display in any way at all the aptitudes, abilities, behavioural characteristics, that put them in the frame to be nurtured and supported, extended and enriched. (Coordinators) give them strategies and training to draw them further into the cultural traits and mores of the middle class that make up the highest percentage in the university population. (Radnor *et al*, 2007:292)

Students so identified and successfully worked with may thus become more middle class in the sense of acquiring some of their social characteristics. But the close-to-academic narratives which are the warp and weft of these characteristics have shored up middle class privilege. Ending such privilege through these means, and extending the ownership of academia, are tasks for social justice, and underpin the realisation of a more socially diverse elite in all spheres in a generation's time. This is a broader notion of social mobility. We should embrace it.

7

The aspirations of 'other' young people: snapshots of the 'disengaged'

There continue to be young people who sometimes remain beyond the reach of services, who do poorly in learning, and who are alienated from their communities. We know that these young people often experience multiple, overlapping problems and risks. (Children's Plan – DCSF 2007:127)

Yeah, I'd just failed in my life. I was really ... I had a feeling I was brought up fine but I was just ... it wasn't me, do you know what I mean? I was, you know, I was putting on an act. *Derek, ex-drug addict, convicted criminal and client of voluntary project*

I used to get discouraged by things ... and by people. *Sally, voluntary project client*

The aspirations of those without aspiration

The process of getting in to prestigious universities may be more fragile for potentially high attaining students from working class backgrounds than for their independent school peers. But life prospects in general for the students at the opposite end of the social and educational spectrum, whom we now consider, the 'disengaged', are brutal, and without intervention, potentially health- and life-threatening.

The social contexts in which these young people live their lives are shown in Figure 3, developed from Figures 1 and 2. School staff, peer group, home, and community are shown similarly as for other students, but the statutory and voluntary agencies are also shown, as they often

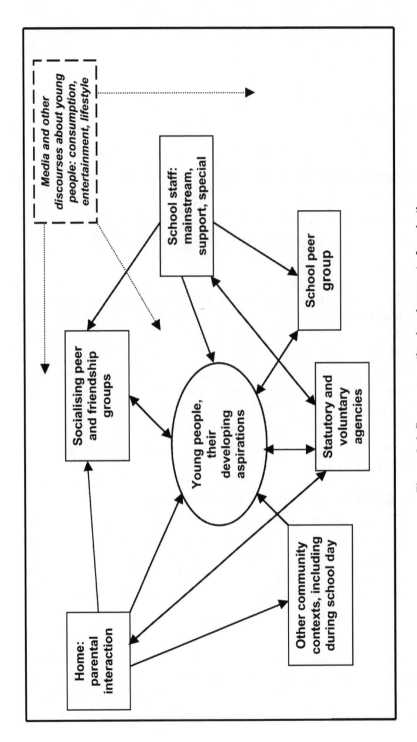

Figure 3: Influences on the development of aspiration in disengaged students, represented by arrows

become a prominent if not always welcome feature of these young people's lives. For them too, these are the sites for the formation, reflection on, and development of, aspiration and aspirational identity. These young people too bring their own embodied dispositions to each of these contexts – the sub-conscious/mental structure by which they iteratively frame and interpret new experiences, their habitus.

But the game for them is radically different from both the silver-spooned managed contexts for independent school pupils and their university-aspirant working class peers. In fact, for them, the narratives about themselves in all these social contexts, with the occasional and possible exception of the agencies, may be increasingly negative with age for any recognised trajectory. And hence they may be mutually re-inforcing in ways which are diametrically the opposite of those for independent school pupils.

The interviews conducted with senior government officials, Connexions and voluntary sector staff illuminate graphically how the cumulative nature of aspirational identity works against these young people developing a positive view of themselves, compounding in their heads the effects of social structure (and fracture). The young people interviewed often gave negative self-views, sometimes speaking about themselves in the past.

In the light of this, it is easy to see why disengaged students may behave in the ways reported. And this evidence, considered alongside national interventions, poses awkward questions for all of us about the quite different nature of the programmes available for disengaged students and the resources invested in them overall.

Who are disengaged young people?

A convincing picture of the nature of current disengagement emerges from UK Government documents. The *Ten Year Strategy for Positive Attitudes* (HM Treasury, 2007) said that the Government's aim was to ensure 'young people's participation in positive activities' (p13), but that:

> ... there remains a small but significant group of young people who are not benefiting from the opportunities that Government has created in the last decade and who need further support to build their resilience against risk. (p12)

The Government's intention therefore was to:

> ...invest significantly ... (in order) to expand the availability of year-round highly-personalised provision for the most disengaged young people, in order to sustain outcomes and progression. (p64)

The aim for 'socially-excluded young people' would be 'to develop the skills and attributes they need to reconnect with mainstream services and succeed in life' (*ibid*, p64).

The Children's Plan, considering young people who are NEET (not in employment, education or training), states that 'low aspirations and low skills have become entrenched' in some areas of industrial decline (DCFS, 2007:114) and goes on to explain that:

> ... as the UK economy continues to adjust, those young people that remain disengaged will become progressively more marginalised, as non-participation is a strong predictor of later unemployment, low incomes, teenage parenthood, depression and poor physical health. (also p114)

Although there may be economic reasons for not being in employment, education or training, therefore, and although not all this group will be disengaged (see below), the personal risks are great. And by the end of the second quarter of 2009 (traditionally the time of year when numbers peak), 11.9 per cent of 16-18 year olds were in the NEET group in England, a figure which is rising (DCSF NEET Statistics Quarterly Brief, available from www.dcsf.gov.uk/rsgateway).

Government's concern has led to a new Public Service Agreement (PSAs are between Central and Local Government, usually on the basis of funding) to 'increase the number of children and young people on the path to success' (*ibid*:126). The relevant indicators included:

– increase(d) participation in positive activities

– reduce(d) ... proportion of young people frequently using illicit drugs, alcohol or volatile substances

– reduce(d) ... under-18 conception rate

– reduce(d) ... number of first-time entrants to the criminal justice system aged 10-17; and

– reduce(d) ... number of 16-18 year olds not in education, employment or training (NEET).

126

within which there would become specific targets for Councils. There will also be:

> ... a new goal that by 2020 all young people will be participating in positive activities to develop personal and social skills, to promote their well-being and to reduce the behaviour that puts young people at risk. (p127)

Finally, in claiming 'great progress in breaking down barriers for young people who are most at risk' (p127), the Children's Plan explained how high the stakes are for the young people described in the header to this Chapter:

> – persistent truants are nearly ten times more likely to be NEET at 16 and four times more likely to be NEET at 18
>
> – young people with emotional and behavioural difficulties are four times more likely to use illicit drugs
>
> – three in five excluded young people report having offended; and
>
> – 71 per cent of young women who are NEET for six months or more between 16-18 years of age are parents by 21. (p127)

So disengaged young people are not accessing services. They may have a history of not going to school, and may have been excluded; they may be NEET, or at risk of it. They may be involved with the criminal justice system; or drug, alcohol or substance abuse; be a teenage parent; or be at risk of some or all of these. They may have no recognised skills, and be unable to succeed.

Some of the students interviewed in 2009, who were clients of a local project of a national voluntary organisation, described their involvement thus:

> I (have) come here to get rid of all my problems. *Pat*
>
> I was in trouble ... up to the usual stuff ... Everything seemed to get messed up somewhere along the line. *Pete*
>
> I('d) done drugs.... It's just everywhere ... I (would) just sit in on my own, doing nothing ... If I did go about with anyone, they just led me astray. *Suze*

And Don did not know, he said, why he was in the project. These expressions of lack of agency – together with those of Derek and Sally at the head of the Chapter – are an important aspect of the disengagement described below. But Derek had become a success story and a volunteer at his project. And Sally, Pat, Pete, Suze and Don were at different stages of trajectories to hopefully becoming so.

The attitudes and behaviours of disengaged young people

Staff interviewed in connection with disengaged students worked in organisations to which young people were referred once they had developed a problem or lost a sense of direction. The young people staff described – like Sally, Pat, Pete, Suze and Don – were therefore all at the heavier end of needs and behaviour, in complete contrast to the young people at independent schools.

The comments reported over the next few pages have many similarities, suggesting these snapshots are representative.

The first comments reported here were made by Connexions staff. Connexions is the statutory organisation set up in the UK to replace the former universal careers service. It is intended to be targeted towards students least likely to stay in education or training, or gain employment, and its professional staff, termed Personal Advisers (PAs), are expected not just to give advice but help young people move on to the next stages of their lives. The funding for this service was returned to local authorities in 2008 (having been removed in 1994), but individual Connexions services, some of which are in the private sector, may now serve several LA areas.

First, who is constructing and telling these stories? A senior official at the then Department for Education and Skills (DfES, now the DCSF) described the vision and expectation of PAs at the 'intensive end', as he termed it, those working with young people most at risk (of being NEET in the first instance):

> It's about personal support, advocacy and brokerage of other services. ... It can be an awful lot of things: ... checking have they got up that morning, ... and gone in to the thing that they're supposed to have. If not, texting them or phoning them. It can be being there for text and phone calls about 'this has happened to me', 'that's happened to me', and it's having the capacity and skills to build a relationship of trust.

> Because ... those sorts of relationships don't happen unless the personal adviser is capable of building that relationship of trust ... And there's a sort of virtuous circle: ... as the trust develops, if the personal adviser is able to

deliver things on behalf of the young people ... the young person has more cause to trust them. So that advocacy is literally ... standing alongside the young person and speaking on their behalf ... helping them to reflect on the issues in their lives, and build the capacity in the young person to take those decisions for themselves, and be able to move on and do things for themselves.

And it is brokerage, acting as a bridge between the young person and other services which they wish to access, like financial support or housing support ... They should be able to address, and help the young person address, any issues in their life which are acting as a barrier to learning and progression; ... be able to challenge and explore around issues of family and aspiration and ... have the technical knowledge to be able to help a young person explore where their interest and capacity can take them, and not to limit it to obvious choices or to the first thing that the young person says.

This is a powerful vision. Targeted PAs are therefore intended to be at the nub of decision and progress making for the disaffected young people they work with. In and outside school, they are likely to be the first to come across disengaged young people before they go on to anything else. I interviewed two of them, Lorna and Arthur. Kevin, the chief executive of the local Connexions service for which they worked, serving four LAs, explained that targeted PAs were workers who

...ideally would probably be working intensively with a group of no more than thirty young people at any one time, probably be meeting up with them anything from a couple of times a week to once every twelve weeks, making contact, and seeing them probably in a café or a youth club, perhaps even in their own home initially. At the toughest end, the work goes on in the young person's home to try and get them to come out and meet them somewhere else. *Kevin, Connexions Chief Executive*

This is redolent of the comments Suze made about herself. Arthur talked about his school age clients thus:

The young people that I work with don't seem to like structure; they work to a different time scale. They don't, even in simple terms ... like getting up at a particular time. They get up when they want to get up, not because they have to ... at seven thirty, eight thirty, nine thirty... They like to have some sort of control over decisions, so: 'not that I have to go to science in five minutes, but I've chosen to go...' *Arthur, Connexions PA*

And Lorna similarly described some of the attitudes she comes across:

> ... they just seem to feel that they don't have to do anything that they don't want to. And that extends into their education: 'if I don't want to go to my lesson, you can't tell me to go'. We used to have those conversations all the time ... It's my choice' – they just don't get it ... (I'll say) 'It's not your choice, because you know it affects your future'... and they just don't seem to grasp that somehow... They think 'I'll just get a job'... (*clicks fingers*) ... or they can get involved in other activities ... Because the NEET group that I'm ... engaging with, they've all been ... young people who basically have been excluded from early college ... or they're involved with the (Youth Offending Team) ... And basically they're just not involved in education and training in any way. *Lorna, Connexions PA*

Arthur described the process whereby some of the students he works with become NEET in similar terms. In his view, this occurs through a lack of self-organisation, sense of reality, or just a plain unwillingness to do anything:

> ...a lot of people end up being NEET because they haven't realised... they're leaving school and they are going to be in this situation when they leave. It's very much a case of 'I'll sort something out later, I'm in school now; when I'm not in school I will do something'. But in reality it's December of year 11, and you have to be applying for things November and December. If you leave it to June or July, everything's full up, so I get a lot of young people that say 'Oh, in September I'll get something'. Some genuinely think that they will in September, others are just fobbing you off and basically saying 'I can't be bothered'. They are the people that will stay NEET because they are voluntarily making themselves NEET. *Arthur, Connexions PA*

In relation to the work she has tried to develop with students, Lorna described the difficulties she had setting up an intensive in-school group to prevent African Caribbean young men becoming NEET (she is African Caribbean herself):

> ...so first of all I had a consultation with each of them. And I think initially there were about twelve and I ended up working with six 'cos the other six decided that it wasn't for them. They were quite happy not to be going to school and they didn't want any support, so they made that decision not to actually attend the group. *Lorna, Connexions PA*

And with the group that did turn up:

> ... even with me as a sort of enabler, and somebody that is actually ... trying to reduce all the barriers to them learning, I would usually have to start each session with 'Can we say good morning?' Do you know what I mean...?

In a similar vein, she gave the example of how a supplementary school had been set up in her area targeting African Caribbean Year 10s and 11s, to help raise achievement. But as it took place on a Saturday, she said, students told her they 'would not go' (and didn't).

Attitudes to future work, career or social trajectory – aspirational identity – varied, but at the stage the PAs were dealing with the young people, none reported specific training or occupational ambitions. Arthur talked about the later and later abandonment of what he called the 'fantasy stage':

> ... in careers terms you go through different stages, and one of those is a sort of fantasy stage ... A lot of (these) young people unfortunately later and later are still in their fantasy stage ...They're convinced they are going to be a professional footballer ... (even by) 14, 15, 16 with some of the young people I deal with. If they play for a very minor club ... they feel that because they belong to a club they could be a professional footballer ... The problem is two fold: there's the ambitions, the fantastical ambitions of young people, because they haven't really had it explained to them properly, what is available to them. And (then also) I don't think they've had enough opportunities to explore what they're capable of... *Arthur, Connexions PA*

This sort of comment has been made before by careers advisers. And it has become common in the educational and other press to talk more generally about young people believing the apparent discourse of such TV shows as the *X factor*. Many young people, according to these accounts, do not expect to have to work hard for success or to be famous (see for example *Hunt for Heroes* in the *TES Magazine*, 10 July, 2009).

Fantasy stage or not, Lorna spoke of apathy, lack of vision and not making a connection between the here and now and what might happen:

> I'm finding that I'm looking at more and more around attitude and low attendance, and basically, like I say, apathy. Just: 'I've got no vision about the future', and where they're going, and why they need to do this school work ... But ... it seems to have more of an impact when it comes to the BME kids ... because there just seems to be a multitude of issues that are affecting them.

Peter, who runs a local community project providing a range of sports-related activities on estates in Yorkshire, also lamented the continuing lack of ambition:

> ...I wouldn't like to generalise, but what I would say is you can definitely see that they are in this ... cycle of, you know ... 'this is where we live, this is where our parents lived'. Parents' aspirations, well certainly a percentage of them, aren't there. It's like ... you know ... 'same as me'.

There is an important difference between having no aspiration and aspirations similar to one's parents', and this is not confined to the disengaged. A similar lack of aspiration was also reported among young people in Bristol compared to those in Birmingham (SHM, 2004) in an LSC-commissioned research report. But it depends on what the parents' aspirations and circumstances are.

Disengaged students' attitudes and behaviours may just be a more developed version of their peers' cool, but the risks have become much greater for them. Once in the NEET group post-16, even entering specific provision (for example, Entry to Employment, E2E, or in some cases where there are low basic skills, pre-E2E) does not mean the young person will leave NEET for good. Kevin, the Connexions Chief Executive, explained that first there is 'single phase NEET', where

> ... it was their first experience, (they were) new to it, possibly (had) been in something already and dropped out or went straight into it after school ... (Then there) is transient NEET. These were young people who had had a number of periods of NEET, gone into something temporary or permanent and dropped out. About 16 per cent of them in that. And then there is the real tough group, consistent NEET – 35 per cent. These were people that spent more time in NEET than not since 16: some concerned about their future, not being able to get back on course, usually with a range of other issues exacerbating their need – trouble with the police, drugs, housing, looked after children...

He further elaborated: '...some of these transient ones and consistent ones just find it impossible to stick with (programmes of learning)'. They are clearly at risk in the terms described in the last section and many will come across Connexions and the organisations interviewed here. And recall this group comprised 11.9 per cent of the age group in summer 2009.

How disengaged self-narratives emerge

These perceived attitudes and behaviours – specifically the apparent indifference or unwillingness to engage with schools or even the agencies visited – will have arisen and developed iteratively in the contexts shown in Figure 3. But given the stage of apparent disaffection reached by these young people, how they present themselves in these contexts will also have helped engender and shape negative perceptions and narratives about them. It will be difficult for these narratives to be constructive by this stage, and when constructive, positively reinforcing.

Communication in the home

Comments about home background were made by several interviewees. Peter, running the community project in West Yorkshire, echoing the engagement difficulty, said:

> ...the young people that we work with... don't sort of engage with mainstream traditional education brilliantly. And they often will come from families who, you know, in terms of sorts of aspirations and role models ... maybe they aren't always there. *Peter, Yorkshire Project*

And similarly, Donald, a local project manager of a national charity dealing with disaffected young people, said:

> ...Often our young people tend to ... have chaotic home lives, and we try and be a stable base for them. *Donald, National Charity*

Lorna, the Connexions PA quoted above, described the difficulties of eliciting any response at all from parents of some of the young people she worked with (like their children of course). None had picked up the phone to find out what she was doing with their children, as she put it. And she reported one young person as saying: 'my mum sends me to school to get an education ... It's not her role to be contacting the school'.

These attitudes to school reflect those reported by Gillies (2007), however, and should not be taken per se to denote lack of interest at home. If the perception of the lack of a communicative relationship at home is accurate, the upshot may be that by the time children are in their teens, parents may perceive they have little influence. And the lack of a communicative relationship with school – between responsible adults in the different contexts of young people's lives – will not enable the type of joint planning which takes place for children attending independent schools. Smooth transition between the social contexts of disengaged young people's lives, with each carrying similar narratives about what they are like, is not possible for them. That their lives may appear more fractured as a consequence and hence, no doubt, more difficult to make sense of, may lie behind some of the comments made about their previous lives by Suze and others, with the detached observation of their own lack of agency.

So the extent of disaffection represented in these young people will reflect the reported lack of positive aspirations in the home, a parental perception of lack of influence, or, at the extreme, the chaos described by Donald. Developed parental ambitions for their children to obtain the better job – or any at all – will therefore be elusive. Compared to being in the homes of children attending independent school, there will be fewer opportunities to communicate and discuss aspirations, articulated into educational and career choices. And the absence of positive, aspirational encouragement in the home may be exacerbated when reportedly some of the young people concerned spend little time there, including at night.

At school

In some cases, young people may disengage from school (just like Willis' lads, 1977), because they cannot see its relevance to their current circumstances. But they may not be disengaged from much else. For example, Arthur described the difficulties faced by some young people in the context of moving away:

> ... A lot of these families are impoverished and the young person is actually supporting the family network. It's not as if they're a separate entity from the family, they're very much a part of the nuclear group there, and they are bringing money (in) ... For some young people I've worked with that means running drugs for a parent ... (so) if the young person goes off to college or university and is removed physically from that situation, they are not going to bring in a sizable chunk of funding which is currently coming in to the home group.

So whether going to college or not is within these young people's horizons, they will find the prosaic routines and structures of Key Stage 3 and 4 life in a comprehensive school in complete contrast to their circumstances at home. They are unlikely to become NEET in the full sense described by Kevin, though their invisible involvement in the alternative economy may make them appear so. They may just become untraceable. This shows how difficult it is to generalise; and school itself may not be the site where disengagement starts.

For others it will be, however, and disengagement may develop in a number of ways. Non-attendance may commence because of early employment outside school, but more likely attendance will begin to drop off because of particular circumstances or dislikes and develop into a habit because of lack of interest, unwillingness to make repeated effort, or the greater effort of re-engaging. Lack of encouragement at home may make this worse, and peer encouragement may eventually reinforce it.

For others still, disengagement at the mild disinterest stage may develop apiece after diagnosis and treatment (or not) of a variety of special needs and conditions, such as ADHD. Treatment may have been in mainstream and special schools, units in and out of school, special placements (eg at a college for key stage 4 for all or part of the week) or personalised programmes. Despite the best intentions of staff, the normative nature of such treatment communicates that something is not right with the student. At its most positive ontologically, this suggests only limited achievement is possible and admirable because of the young person's circumstances. If this limitation of aspiration is not internalised and embraced, then resignation may gently sap into disengagement.

At the same time, the difficulties in interpersonal communication between adults in the different social contexts of the young people's lives will be compounded by the increasingly fractured nature of the educational provision made for them. Young people will find an increasing number of services and professionals have an interest in them, and however successful Every Child Matters has been locally, this will make communication and coherence more complex, putting an extra responsibility on the young people themselves that they may not comprehend or be able to fulfill.

In the mainstream school itself, the positive iterative communications which scaffold aspirational identity for many students will become negative when faced with developing disengagement. And whatever their academic capacity, these young people will not help schools deliver their performance targets, particularly as these multiply in urban settings. They will not see themselves as, or be told that they are, important pupils for their school. Quite the contrary. The most important message they will take on, because of the regulation of the performativity culture (see, for example, Ball 2008:43/4), is that they are a problem. They are failures. This message will become more persistent if they are disruptive and attract attention from pastoral staff who, in 2009, may no longer have a teaching background.

But these young people will know what successful students are like and who they are, while their own suggested educational trajectories appear correctional rather than aspirational. Their developing self-narratives will be suffused with the realisation that they are unlikely to be successful in any normative sense whatsoever. Whatever aspirational identities they do develop will be different from ones recognised, rewarded and paraded in school.

Peer group

In these circumstances, it is only human that some of these young people will find or seek out a similar peer group in an effort to find positive reinforcement – again like Willis' lads (1977, and see below). The group they find may articulate and reinforce their common identity through their own narratives and behaviours (this has long been known, see for example, Sewell, 1997), which themselves will be iteratively self-accruing.

Lorna described a group of African Caribbean students she had worked with who told her as a group that their disaffection began in Year 10 when they had no Maths teacher. It made them feel, according to the group, that the teachers did not care about them, so they did not want to make an effort in school.

The peer group they find may be on the fringe of mainstream school, or may already be active resisters in a more segregated setting. Others may be non-attenders like them, people to hang around with when not in school. Others again, like the loners described by Kevin who do not often emerge from their homes, will find themselves in the company of similar people, when they finally make it to statutory or voluntary services. Everyone referred to special treatment will find a new community of peers. Discovering a reengagement narrative is more difficult.

In the community

In all these cases, young people are now mixing with a peer group with reverse-normative aspirational identities, progressively assumed and sometimes articulated. The self-accruing attitudes and behaviour will carry over into their contacts with the community, engendering further negative reactions; hence the contact with the criminal justice system and the 'criminality' referred to by Peter and others below. These continual iterative contacts in the community and peer group scaffold aspirational identities quite different from those of the independent school students. Social structure works to keep them where they are, as it did for Willis' lads.

Experiences in wider working class communities will vary. Even the most socially disadvantaged communities are not uniformly so, despite their exoticisation in much of the written and broadcast media. Families do stay together and have aspirations even after the closure of a major employer in an area, though sustaining them may become progressively more difficult if they cannot find and take up employment for themselves, however insecure. Such parents will have expectations of their children. It is these families on local authority estates who are most likely to enter the education market, in an attempt to climb a few places up the stratified school (and, of course, social) system.

The balance of positive aspirations and ways of living in communities will affect how self-narratives of young people develop, and what they see as socially important. Their micro-experiences will be nuanced and vary street by street. Anti-social behaviour, in which some will be involved, will elicit community responses that inform their self-perceived social trajectories as bad, or wrong, or devil-may-care, and outraged local media coverage will exacerbate this.

Media narratives of success

Meanwhile, none of these young people will be able to escape the denotations of success in our consumer society in the written and broadcast media, even if their internet use is light. Consumption messages are all round them, particularly in urban areas, and they are narrated on television and in DVD drama. The denotations of the good life – money, decent cars, designer clothing, and respect from peers and others – have become inaccessible to them by normative routes, something they will have been told repeatedly throughout their lives.

People like them do not have these things legally. Post fantasy stage, their self-perceived, but maybe rarely articulated, aspirational identities will not include them. Some will begin to include other activities and outcomes, many with destructive consequences for themselves and others. They will subliminally embrace and pursue the risks described in the Government documents.

This is one interpretation of gun and knife crime. Involvement in petty criminality (Peter and others) to provide daily necessities or some of the symbols of the comfortable life can lead to induction to the drugs trade, whose local agents and traders, some being slightly older peers, will be well known locally and easy to contact. Such involvement can provide access to bling at an early age: desirable rewards, with apparently little effort, and without all the difficulties and personal challenges they may face though an educational route to success.

As Donald, the project manager working with the disaffected, said, echoing Arthur's comments on page 134, and those of Peter:

> Where there's a lot of dealing going on, a lot of that sort of stuff, they see... it's a quick way to get money by getting involved in criminality.

Cultures of resistance: the lads and lasses of 2010

There are thus huge historical, structural, social, economic and pedagogical realities behind the behaviours and attitudes of disengaged young people. What is striking from all these accounts is their counternormative nature, similar to that found in Phil Willis' descriptions of the 'lads' (Willis, 1977), finally explored here in more detail.

The 'lads' were a group of teenage men expecting to join their fathers, after leaving their midlands comprehensive school, in manual factory jobs that put a premium on physical strength. The lads lived a culture of fighting, sexual precocity, resisting school expectations and 'having a laff', often at the expense of other pupils (for example, the 'ear 'oles'), who had more elevated aspirational identities and saw the connection with doing well at school.

This lived culture, according to Willis, was a mirror image of that on the factory floor and manual work generally. Although the narratives about themselves these young men received from school were largely negative, as Willis explains, similar to disengaged young people today, their lived culture, and the expectation of what would come after school, were positive and supported specific aspirational identities reinforced by peer group and fathers (leaving aside here the role of their families and gender expectations in their socialisation). These young men anticipated trajectories which included getting a job, having girlfriends, getting married and settling down.

The attitudes and behaviours of disengaged students described in this Chapter can similarly be understood as part of a resistance culture in the social contexts in Figure 3 where otherwise they would constantly receive the message of failure. Resistance enables them to rebrand their failure positively.

But herein lies a great difference. Willis' lads had a positive self-recognised trajectory through manual work, despite school resistance, but these sorts of manual jobs in manufacturing were largely to disappear over the next twenty years or so after Willis was writing and with them the clear occupational trajectories for unqualified young men in many communities. Although Lynn Raphael Reed and her colleagues found in their study that easily available casual unskilled jobs had reemerged in south Bristol, making the pursuit of further education or training similarly a less attractive option for some students (Raphael Reed *et al*, 2007), including well-qualified ones, this is not the case everywhere. Nor do these newer jobs either replace the extent of previous employment or provide the same sociable work setting in which masculinities can be acted out and solidarities created.

And in the 10 per cent most deprived workless neighbourhoods from which many disengaged students come, 33 per cent of heads of household were unemployed well into the last economic recovery, and 29 per cent of adults overall were still economically inactive (ODPM, 2004). Two years after these figures, another Government-commissioned report was saying:

Changes in the nature and organisation of work have led to increased uncertainty, fluidity and insecurity in labour markets, which are characterised by a greater degree of segmentation and inequality, both socially and spatially. High levels of unemployment and inactivity have become entrenched amongst certain groups and in certain areas, and there has been an increasing focus on the mismatch between high levels of worklessness in deprived neighbourhoods and employment growth in areas peripheral to major urban centres. (Sanderson, 2006)

By 2009, the number of people in workless households was rising again, up by 10 per cent from the previous year (Labour Force Survey, available from www.statistics.gov.uk), potentially entrenching and deepening the social and economic circumstances. For the disengaged and everyone else, this means that a generally available trajectory of sociable, manual work for the unqualified will never return, even on a casual basis.

What in other circumstances might be a modest and sensible aspiration of wanting to be like one's parents, may thus lead in these communities to serial casual employment at its best, or as likely as not, unemployment, serial unemployment, and the risks dwelt upon. In these circumstances, resistance is about dignity, self-respect and sanity; about remaining a human being.

The development of aspirational identities of disengaged students

Another area of consensus emerging from the interviews was what appeared to work with disengaged students. This was not a systematic survey of practice, of course, but again, these indications from what are often committed, pragmatic, generous and informal ways of working with young people in different parts of the country are likely to be found elsewhere. The comments from the young people interviewed also reflected what staff said.

The targeted PAs related anecdotes of how successful referrals from their own groups or clients to various, mainly voluntary sector, agencies, had led to small successes (for example, on a Level 1 vocational course at a local college). These had helped with the development of a sense of trajectory, an incipient aspirational identity, where before there was none.

All interviewees said that the process of working with disengaged students must begin with talking to them sympathetically about what they want to do and be, as opposed to invoking the discursive practice whereby the failures they had been and would remain are marked up. Necessarily, because of the extent of disengagement, this sometimes took extended time and patience to convince the young person they were being listened to.

For them, it was about having a 'sense of knowing that there's somebody out there to talk to, that somebody cares' (Lorna). This should provide the basis for a sound 'relationship with both the young people and the wider community. If you get their trust and build that relationship, then I think it opens a lot of doors' (Peter).

The young people interviewed perceived this process as staff being 'friendly' (Pat, Sally), 'being on the same level as the students' (Pat), the project being 'like a family' (Pat, Sally) and 'something to look forward to', and about beginning to 'feel much better about myself' (Suze). These comments also probably reflect the more informal approaches of youth work.

But the involvement is about 'moving them on' to different stages of a trajectory, as a number of staff interviewees said, identifying what could be available to them and what they would need to do to achieve it. As Peter says,

> ...when I was growing up, it was very similar ... It took someone to sort of say, 'Well, why can't you do that? There is no reason why you can't do it'. And I think that is still lacking for a lot of young people. And then, you know ... sometimes it's (just) the simple life. They think, 'Oh, there is something there that I can do. I'm good at that'. But they need a little push.

His feeling was that some of the young people he worked with had not yet received that push. This was echoed by Donald, the project manager, but the push has to be done in the right way:

> ... in order to help young people move on you've got to be able to sort of say: 'What do you want? You know, you can do x'. Especially when they see our staff who come from that background. So: 'I was like you but I've got a job, you know, I'm doing this and that'. That really helps.

But this is not straightforward:

> It might take a long time with an outreach worker who will really be able to begin to sort of dig down...

It also requires positive attitudes, which are a feature of this work:

> ... because I guess generally we sort of believe at heart that most young people don't really want to be in the situations they're in, be excluded.

So the consensus was that, for many of these young people (but not all of them), being able to talk properly to someone recognisably like them is important, irrespective of their qualifications, as Donald said. This is the social structural mirror inverse of the independent school students' situation. Donald further elaborated:

> ...what helps (here) as well is that two of my staff are very much ex-clients, they're from that background, you know; they've had difficult upbringings themselves, they make it sort of more acceptable.

Echoing Peter:

> ...all the staff are sort of local people and a lot of them are from the communities we work in, which is again, you know: 'This is on the map, this opportunity is really within your grasp and, you know, have a go at it'. *Peter, Yorkshire Community Project*

In addition, staff are not implicated in the schools or services which have given a negative message to these young people, and which have been resisted as a consequence. Peter again:

> Certainly I think ... one of the reasons ... we are successful is that we are not seen as a 'doing to' organisation. We aren't statutory services or an education department. We are not the council, if you like – a bit neutral – so sometimes it's easier for us to get into places that statutory services can't. *Peter, Yorkshire*

Peter gave an example of how all this works through a success story:

> ... we recruited some staff a couple of years ago. One of the staff we took on was a young 16/17 year old lad ... His mum was so shocked that we had sort of taken him on (*laughter*) and given him this opportunity ... He's probably from one of our rougher estates if you like, but his age, I suppose, to us is not a big deal. You know he's a young lad, very sort of keen and vibrant and he's great – he's already in great touch with some of the young people that we work with. Again, his age is so close to some of the young people, that you can see why he's a great role model for them ... You have to find a way of talking to young people... so it's trying to find something in common.

But helping young people move on also means helping the development of

> ...action plans, (and) goal setting... (in order to) start their... first steps down the path of personal development...in order that they can (go) on to employment, education, further training, volunteering, that sort of side of things.
> *Donald*

The best location for such work, on the same principle, according to Genevieve, the head of policy at another prestigious national charity that funds many projects for disaffected young people, is therefore 'close to, but not on, the local authority estates'.

The diverse needs of disaffected young people, and their very individual paths to this stage, require these organisations to exercise patience in their 'digging down' as Donald described it. And all have to be flexible in how and when they work with young people. Kevin, the Connexions chief executive, reflecting on referrals, explains:

> ... (some young people) can get in (to provision), but they don't seem to be able to continue, and therefore it's how you can help them to stick in there and go forward ... which is sometimes getting the provider to be more flexible, and certainly getting the young person to recognise that, if you start not attending and being late, the end point of this is they won't put up with you.

The charity Donald works for keeps on taking young people back, no matter how many times they do not turn up, until they make progress, and then, later, encourages them to move on again when they need to, to avoid getting too comfortable.

Particular events or changes in life circumstances – irrespective of the services they are accessing – could also lead to changes in how some young people see themselves and how they can be worked with. Derek, whose quotation heads this Chapter, is a good example. He had had a former history of drug abuse and had spent time in prison for aggravated assault. One day, he said, he just saw himself differently, that 'he'd just failed in his life ... It wasn't a very big thing, not really. One of my best friends died of an overdose'.

He began to work as a volunteer in the Yorkshire community project. At the time of the interview he had recently begun to work on a more permanent basis and had just attained his first football referee's certificate

– the first time he had passed anything. I asked about his self-confidence returning:

> ... that's right, yes it did, yeah, and I really liked the jobs that I did, do you know what I mean? And I wanted to make a difference for the kids and stuff.

A number of staff interviewees mentioned taking on ex-clients as volunteers. Suze, one of the young people interviewed, also had such an ambition.

Summary and commentary: making provision for disengaged students

The disengaged will always be with us; the 11.9 per cent figure is nearly one in eight after all, and has never been zero, even in prosperous times. The complex processes by which disengagement arises and develops are rooted in social economic, political and psychological circumstances outside the school, which must be addressed to achieve change. And schools too are also deeply implicated: the pedagogies offered to young people in the statutory and post-16 education system need to be addressed.

So even if levels of disengagement may be whittled down in the medium to long term, there will remain a need for the work described here with young people whose disengagement may still put them at risk. Largely, this involves supporting a transition, often intense, often interrupted, to some form of supported training and employment.

It is easy to understand the longstanding presence of charities in this field. They have a history of successful work with young people who require the more informal approaches of staff often recruited from unusual backgrounds, and who value the independence of working outside the statutory sector. The availability of this provision complements and enhances the work with young people of Connexions PAs, who recognise their need for further work before entering education, employment or training.

Relying on such projects and charities, with these strengths, nevertheless entails that provision will vary by area, and individual projects will have something to offer some young people and not others. There is only one project such as Peter's, for example, and it happens to be in Yorkshire. The Local Government Association (LGA/CSJ, 2009) lists other such projects in various locations, all seemingly individual in their circumstances.

The maintenance of these projects also depends on the funding available locally. Interviewees in the charities reported referrals from a variety of sources: schools, Local Authorities (placement officers, behaviour support staff, education welfare officers, psychologists, and social workers), the police, and occasionally from local Learning and Skills Councils (LSC) at that time. Referrals did not always come with funding, but nevertheless charities could often see they had something to offer the young people concerned. They had to spend time fund-raising themselves from prominent individuals, other charities, other LA departments sometimes, companies and ordinary members of the public. For small community projects, this meant living from hand to mouth from time to time.

Even when referrals were funded, or there were more general funding agreements, projects often had to respond to LA requirements that had been changed after consultations in which they had not been involved. Worse, often overwhelmed LA Placement Officers struggling to find something to meet a young person's needs would sometimes refer to a project that happened to be there, rather than what was needed in the charities' view. According to Donald,

> ... LEAs were dumping young people they didn't know what to do with on (us), and saying 'you deal with them, we've not got a school place for them'... We would have young people coming to us, and great, we could do great work with them, but we didn't have anywhere to move them on to.

None of this is satisfactory. In contrast to young people at the other end of the social spectrum of need/ability, the gifted and talented, there has been no national strategy or systematic investment in organisations working with disengaged students. There needs to be. Even where government funding has set up major local projects in socially disadvantaged areas, such as the New Deal for Communities (NDC), there appears to have been little systematic investment.

Funding is expected in NDC and other regeneration schemes to complement statutory provision, and be driven by a local community vision. There are many NDC projects nationally to help *disadvantaged* students attain higher while at school, according to one of the national

145

evaluators I interviewed. Some of them are of very high quality according to her and do make complementary provision (for example, for family literacy and encouraging parental involvement). But overall the result is difficult to detect (CRESR, 2005) for disengaged students. In addition, some of these voluntary projects existed before NDC and used the funding to expand.

However, Children's Trusts are now expected to commission a proportion of their services through the third sector (HM Treasury, 2007) and this opportunity should be taken to provide more secure funding agreements with valued local charitable providers. They should be part of a local patchwork of services which together are able to mitigate the many risks these young people may face. Being able to respond informally when appropriate, and together provide prompt treatment as the need arises, would be tantamount to interfering in social structure to provide better sustenance for the development of disengaged young peoples' positive aspirations. Their prospects otherwise will remain the worst in our society.

8

Social Justice and the State

Looking at social class differences in the standards of institutions provides a vocabulary for understanding inequality. It highlights the ways in which institutional standards give some people an advantage over others as well as the unequal ways that cultural practices in the home pay off in settings outside the home. Such a focus helps to undercut the middle class presumption of moral superiority over the poor and working class. A vocabulary of social structure and social class is vastly preferable to a moral vocabulary that blames individuals for their life circumstances. Annie Lareau (2003:257)

Inequalities of circumstance and opportunity

In this last Chapter, I return to inequalities of circumstance in the UK, which continue despite the mixed progress over the past ten years or so (Hills *et al*, 2009). I consider optimistically the circumstances in which the structural disadvantages experienced by working class families, in the sense of disproportionate denial of access of their children to future wealth and power, can be diminished and overcome. And connected with this, I examine the developing emphasis in public service reform from 2008 onwards of promoting social mobility. I argue that, irrespective of whether the state is large or small, only the use of its power can modify institutions which shore up generational advantage.

Attitudes towards addressing these twin inequalities – of circumstance and opportunity – appear to have been hardening recently. A survey conducted for the Sutton Trust by Ipsos MORI in 2008 found that three out of four people think that income differences in Britain are too large (Sutton Trust/Ipsos MORI, 2008) and that seven in ten (only slightly less) also believed that parents' income plays too big a part in determining children's life chances. As this book was being finalised, the Charity Commissioners were enforcing public service tests on independent schools which had been long left alone, despite the tax advantages of charitable status.

Two arguments about social mobility

There are two arguments to be made about social mobility. The first is about whether children now are more or less likely than a generation ago to be able to improve on the circumstances of their parents. This is about social improvement rather than the reproduction with which much of this book has been concerned; being able to attain the 'better jobs' central to UK Government thinking (Cabinet Office, 2008b, 2009a).

Generally speaking, the possibility of improvement has diminished in recent years. The post-war generation born in the 1950s benefited from a huge expansion of the middle class bureaucracies in the public and private sectors (Riddell, 2003). Structural and economic change allowed the absorption of more people into better jobs from wider backgrounds, without demanding that an equivalent number of other people should relinquish theirs.

In numerical terms, of the generation born in 1958, 31 per cent of men in the lowest income quartile had fathers in the same bracket, while 35 per cent of men in the highest quartile did so. For the generation born in 1970, however, these two figures had become 35 per cent and 42 per cent respectively. In other words, social groupings were becoming more stable from one generation to the next. It was becoming harder for young men from working class backgrounds to elevate their occupational position, and less likely in the professional classes that they would reduce theirs (Blanden, Gregg and Machin, 2005). This still meant that more than three quarters of those working class men born in 1958 were able to obtain better jobs, and more of them did so from unskilled backgrounds, but this had reduced to two thirds of those born in 1970 (Woods *et al*, 2003).

These reducing figures for relative social mobility (from one generation to the next) put the opportunities in the UK ahead of the US, but behind those in West Germany (figures before reunification), Finland, Canada,

Denmark, Sweden and Norway (Blanden, Gregg and Machin, 2005). The figures for women are better, but reflect changing social expectations and developing occupational structures, on which I will not dwell here.

This brings us to the second argument about mobility. Using the registrar general's class scheme which applied until 2001, and leaving aside the association between social class and attainment (Power *et al*, 2002), for both the 1958 and the 1970 cohorts, it was eight times more likely that the son of a father in social class I would have a job in social class I or II than the son of a father in social class V. So although many people in the UK were still able to better the circumstances of their parents, change for the vast majority of people was rarely dramatic, with most occupational moves (up and down) being to adjacent social categories (Woods *et al*, 2003). Accelerated rises through social classes – from rags to riches or the other way round – are exceptional.

As time goes on, the greater numbers in the more elevated social positions made it more difficult for people to be continually promoted to them (Blanden and Machin, 2007), without enforcing demotion on others, as the newer social and occupational structure solidified. So this second argument is about *elite recruitment* – to the heights of the major professions and transnational corporations (see Brown *et al*, 2008 and Panel on Fair Access, 2009). The elites – the heights of our economy, polity and society – are not open equally to all. Merit – and being bright – has a social basis.

And passing on recruitment from one generation to another is precisely what the managed model of social reproduction, and the relationship of independent schools and prestigious universities shores up (see Chapter 4). The choice of independent school should be seen for what it is – the choice of social and occupational trajectory. The difficulty of continual new recruitment to higher social strata is compounded by the structures used by people already there to ensure they pass on their acquired advantages to their children, not somebody else's. And this includes the way that middle class parents strategise exclusively and use their advantage in the market in state school places (Riddell, 2003; Ball, 2003a).

So, although there is some evidence that there has been an increase in the quality of jobs available since 2000, measured by a number of factors (Cabinet Office, 2008b: 22), public sector reform, and the changes accompanying and resulting from it, need to be judged against both these arguments for social mobility, not just one of them.

Three methods of addressing the two arguments: disrupt, reconstruct, expand

There are three pathways to providing the types of mobility each of the two arguments advocates.

The first is to *disrupt* the functioning of the entrenched social structures described in this book, constructed round independent schools, and the market in state school places. The second is to *reconstruct* the opportunities and pathways to mobility that are not available to working class students, because of the exclusive functioning of the managed model of social reproduction, the difficulty of developing and sustaining different aspirational identities, and the inequalities in schooling systems partly created by the market. For this second pathway to be successful, besides addressing what happens in schools and classrooms, the non-school social contexts of working class children's lives need to be able to function in ways analogous to those of middle class students. The third is to *widen* the proportion of professional and managerial jobs available in the economy and alter the ways that professions and organisations recruit and promote.

Prospects for change: disruption

There are no immediate prospects of disrupting the managed model as far as independent schools are concerned, either by dramatic changes to their social intake or changing the relationship with prestigious universities.

There will be no systemic expansion of bursaries at independent schools, for example, no matter how generous alumni and other fee paying parents may be and however insistent the Charity Commissioners. Any such expansion could not rival the availability of the former Assisted Places Scheme and it has long been known that even this scheme did not enable the wide-ranging recruitment of working class students (Fitz *et al*, 1986). Insistence on bursaries will have no real effect on the current structure of opportunities, an expansion of the en-nobling process described in Chapter 5, no more, and certainly not a systemic one. And in itself, such an expansion would not help create the symbiotic drip feeds at home and school described in Chapters 3 and 4 which are central to the achievement of places at prestigious univer-sities.

Leaving Professor Richards' comments aside, the apparent desire of the prestigious universities visited for this book to widen the social basis of their intakes is more promising. And so is that of others, to judge from their public comments. But there are huge obstacles in the way.

The first is that a much higher proportion of candidates for prestigious universities will present with the required predicted three A grades dis-cussed in Chapter 6. The Joint Council for Qualifications (reported in BBC News, 20 August, 2009) said that 50 per cent of A Level entries from independent schools were awarded this top grade in 2009, while overall this figure is about a quarter. And the independent sector provides up to 20 per cent of entries at A Level overall (Panel on Fair Access, 2009). For significant change, there would need to be a more finely-grained differentiation of candidates, as Malcolm advocated in Chapter 6, through the examination system itself rather than its being supple-mented by extra tests susceptible to coaching, and a systemic willing-ness of prestigious universities to make differential offers depending on the school context. There must be doubts about whether a new A* grade will make much difference to this, but even if it does, to be systemic, all this requires government pressure. An invitation to consider develop-ments in university admissions practice may be promising and inclu-sive, but it will not bring about systemic change, even when allied to the current benchmarks, as we have seen.

The second obstacle is that the closeness of independent schools to prestigious universities is not just maintained by the drip feed process, links maintained by heads of subject departments, and the similarity of their buildings, but by the similarities of discourse between home, school and admissions procedures described in Chapter 6. Given it is unlikely that notions of academic potential will change, and even less likely that the structure and expectations of three year bachelor degrees in academic subjects will do so, this requires intervention in working class students' social contexts. The prospects are more promising here and are more about reconstruction, discussed in the next section.

Abolition or systemic reform of the school places market, the other mechanism critical to maintaining middle class social advantage, through the facility to engage effectively with the admissions process and ability to buy homes in areas served by favoured schools, seems similarly unlikely. Reform to date has been about regulating the market, or tinkering largely. Making the code of practice statutorily binding, prohibiting parental interviews and seeking to combat fraudulent parental claims are about making the market more efficient or fair, without tackling the exacerbation of school stratification which under-pins social inequality (Riddell, 2003, 2007). In fact, rulings from the school adjudicator (the person in England with the power to decide on school admissions procedures when there is conflict between in-terested parties) to allow banded ability in intakes to some secondary schools, in addition to those of Academies such as Mossbourne in Hackney, will disadvantage many neighbouring urban schools, creating deeper bottom strata (Riddell, *ibid*).

The fact is that preventing the social sifting process of the market re-quires reducing the scope for middle class agency, either by perhaps using allocation processes such as random lotteries, initially introduced in two areas in Brighton in 2003, or returning to the school place alloca-tions made by local authorities before 1982. Though an argument can be made for both these developments, because the current allocations system magnifies social inequality (Riddell, 2003), their introduction flies in the face of the rhetoric of the empowered citizen consumer. It is unimaginable that any UK Government will make such a change. We will be left with tinkering.

And the outright abolition of private schooling is hardly even worth discussing. It would run counter to all social policy in the UK since the Second World War. It would be countered by vested interests using a misapplied narrative of excellence, rather than naming the main-tenance and reproduction of social advantage – which is what such a large private sector in the UK really represents – for what it is. Actually, given the relatively small proportion of the electorate that decides which government is in power in the UK, because of the number of seats which has to change hands, any such radical proposals would be rejected by any political party intending to maintain a broad coalition of voters.

The prospects for disrupting the social reproductive mechanisms of middle class families, in the interests of greater social justice, are therefore poor and attention is better paid to the reconstruction and expansion of opportunities available elsewhere. Besides being more productive, this is also where most Government reforms have been focused.

Prospects for change: reconstruction of (new) opportunities

As was argued in Chapter 6, a wide range of policy interventions in the UK could be considered to have contributed to raising, sustaining, and enabling the realisation of higher aspirations in working class students. All of the standards based reform could be included, as could the historic urban interventions such as Excellence in Cities, and the attempts to broaden the basis for achievement and well being in family and community through Every Child Matters.

New Opportunities, the first white paper to be published specifically on increasing social mobility (Cabinet Office, 2009a), runs through all these reforms and others to proclaim what has been done so far. It has Chapters on the early years, 'world class schools', and 'pathways for all' (on the reforms of further and higher education). A more detailed outline of government education policy is contained in the latest schools white paper *Your child, your schools, our future* (DCSF, 2009), but much of it is themed on social mobility. The Government recognises, accurately, that none of this is finished work, and probably could never be.

New Opportunities includes other, newer developments focused on schools serving working class communities. One is the development of a 'bespoke school-based course of CPD to support the whole school workforce in meeting the challenges of a school with high numbers of disadvantaged pupils' (p53), as part of a section on getting the 'most effective teachers into the most challenging schools'. I have argued elsewhere that these schools, usually in the bottom strata of urban school systems, are individual in their circumstances, requiring individually community-related visions and missions, rather than formulaic approaches to teaching and leadership (Riddell, 2003, 2007). So there is a possibility here, though it remains to be seen whether such an approach is consistent with other aspects of the current performativity framework for such schools, such as the new Ofsted inspection grading system or the so-called National Challenge (see Chapter 6 and Riddell, 2009, for more on this).

The other is the dissemination of the 'lessons from *The Extra Mile Project*' (p54) which ran for the academic year 2008/9 in secondary schools and was based on the DCSF's own advisers' research into schools in challenging areas which were 'bucking the trend', as the DCSF website says. It is considered part of the 'narrowing the gap' agenda (of attainment between children from different social backgrounds). Schools were given twelve activities to try. This may be a positive project, particularly if schools are invited to consider its findings in relation to their own contexts. And intriguingly in relation to the points made earlier about the use of language to maintain advantage and make the metaphorical journey shorter to prestigious university for independent school pupils, the briefing paper for the *Extra Mile* project (DCSF, 2008d) also says 'effective schools provide pupils with a range of formal and informal language repertoires, both spoken and written' (p30). Allied to the notion held by Radnor *et al*'s (2007) gifted and talented school coordinators of inducting working class students into middle class thought habits, this could provide the basis for wider strata of society *owning* academic discourse.

The two directly relevant current major interventions focused on widening the social basis of university admissions, the Gifted and Talented Programme and AimHigher, have been considered in detail in Chapter 5. While they can together form a coherent programme for some students, this is not yet universally available, and the process of aspiration formation in general remains fragile, depending as it does on supremely effective agency at all levels of the education system. This is why I argued that the results of these programmes will be to provide a newly ennobled stream of working class students to universities, who will require personal qualities not needed by their independent school peers, but not in itself systemic change.

New Opportunities intends to deepen and extend the focus of such programmes. Reiterating the connection between attainment and social background, and of a 'community effect' on aspiration in one of its background papers (Cabinet Office, 2008c), *New Opportunities* includes proposals for the development of a universal scheme to 'identify young people with the potential to achieve at university from low-income backgrounds early and ensure they receive a package of structured assistance across their time at secondary school' (p62/3). The extension of the City Gates scheme, to help achieve this end, was later announced as part of the 2009 proposals for developing gifted and talented provision.

The intention is that this new scheme 'will be as comprehensive as that often received by young people attending the best schools and colleges with high rates of progression to higher education' and will include 'support to attend the most selective institutions' (p63). This scheme will begin with 'early experience' and include attendance at schools 'with structural links to a university', presumably trusts. The Government intends to have this in place by 2012. Such a scheme could over time put in place the advice considered lacking in state schools by Tamsin (see Chapter 6) and, potentially, at one step removed, widen the social basis of elite recruitment.

And this scheme will be complemented by the provision of a personal tutor from 2010 for every secondary pupil, who 'knows them well, checks progress and responds quickly if any problems emerge' (p48). It remains to be seen whether this will be substantially different from sometimes indifferent tutoring, but the possibility of another social context in school, through discussions with a tutor, could give rise to positive narratives and self-narratives. It could help, if envisioned and implemented appropriately, the development of a drip feed.

Such developments will begin to reconstruct social contexts in school to support and foster the development of aspirational identities that include university. City Gates type provision, if eventually available to all young people who could go to prestigious universities, will also deepen the important alternative peer group described in Chapter 5 and shown in Figure 2. Potentially, it might also affect the preparation and understanding of even supportive parents.

There are three other interventions described in *New Opportunities* which might help affect the aspirational basis in family and community in the medium to long term. The first is the setting up of the National Equality Panel, intended to look at how 'factors such as who you are interact with your social and family background to affect life chances' (p22) – a recognition of the nature of aspirational identity, and what could be done to intervene. Further, this has been chaired by John Hills, whose work has been quoted in this book. The Panel had stopped taking evidence but had not reported at the time of writing.

The second is the development of Inspiring Communities, a project to be based initially in fifteen areas, where neighbourhoods will be 'invited to design and deliver a package of interventions for young people, their families and communities'. Inspiring Communities will be 'places where schools, businesses, local agencies, parents and the wider community all believe that their young people can succeed, and where they can work together to help them achieve their aspirations'. This is a different ambition from the possibility of all public services working together in an area, contained in the second working paper (Cabinet Office, 2008c), and advocated in my last book, *Schools for Our Cities* (Riddell, 2003). But a managed project, with the 11-14 focus identified in the same working paper, will present the possibility of real evidence of how this could work. For university progression, however, these projects will need to be envisioned and implemented appropriately.

The third, while possibly having an effect on progression to university, is more likely to enable the development of appropriate provision for young people who might become NEET. In the light of Kevin's reported comments on its current cycling and recycling, this is tricky, especially in a recession. But the planned extension of the current 65 'Family Intervention Projects' (*New Opportunities*, p87), intended for families 'with poor parenting... (and which have) education and learning problems such as truancy, exclusion or bad behaviour', may in the long run help the situations which engender the disengagement described in Chapter 7.

These pragmatic, step by step reforms are to be welcomed and encouraged. Those implementing them need to understand their potential for educational, social and occupational trajectories, however, by providing a different social context outside school. Inspiration may become transformation in the long term, but even then not everywhere. For now, bringing on more students with aspirations from working class backgrounds, while leaving the mechanisms for passing on middle class advantage intact, requires them to have the extra personal qualities described in Chapter 5, that is, for them to be even better in order to succeed. Even if all these interventions are successful, working class students will not be competing equally. And so the solution – and a major dependency of government proposals – is the creation of more opportunities.

Prospects for change: expansion of professional and managerial positions and widening opportunities for promotion

New Opportunities (Cabinet Office, 2009a) is premised first on widening access to better jobs through the policy interventions described: increasing social mobility by increasing educational levels, progression, and training accessibility. But it is also premised on the expansion of economic opportunities. Part of this is to do with global developments, in the terms of the narrative alluded to in Chapter 5:

> Over the next two decades, new customers, production patterns, technologies and expectations are all set to generate enormous opportunities for jobs, businesses and even new industries. (*New Opportunities*, Cabinet Office, 2009a:15)

Positive economic prospects for the UK include the expansion of the new global middle class (a market for our exports), to more than a billion 'within a couple of decades' (p15); new technology-driven change; more efficient global supply chains to provide 'opportunities in the knowledge-intensive industries in which we excel, such as research and development and specialist manufacturing and business services' (*ibid*); the development of low-carbon industries; and increasing expectations for personalised services.

But the Government also considers it has a role in *realising* these opportunities – they cannot be left to the development of global markets. So the white paper also explains what the Government is doing to encourage business development, innovation and enterprise, broadband accessibility, new environmental industries and general economic development. The intentions overall behind the white paper are to:

- position the UK economy to benefit from emerging global opportunities

- help build up everyone's capabilities and unlock their talents, throughout their lives, so they can take advantage of these opportunities; and

- ensure that the families and communities in which people develop are best able to support them to realise their potential (p20)

The latter point echoes mine about aspirational identity.

The final report of the Fair Access to the Professions Panel (Panel on Fair Access, 2009), which was commissioned as a consequence of *New Opportunities*, also assumes that its ambitions to 'expand the pool of talent' (p6) and for 'unleashing aspiration' (p7 and its title) can be realised on the basis that there will be up to seven million more professional and managerial jobs by 2020 (based on a submission made to the panel by the Sutton Trust).

No further comment will be made here about economic policy. Leaving aside disagreement about how the recession that started in 2008 may develop and end, it cannot be assumed that all the new opportunities will land in the UK, or that they will usher in a wider-based high skill high wage economy.

But, perhaps because it is a commissioned report rather than a statement of government policy, the Fair Access Panel's report is much franker and more open about intentions. It most certainly does not want to interfere with what I have termed the managed model of social reproduction; it does not want to see 'bright people lose out' (p45), for example. However, although in that sense the report may not be seen as socially challenging, what it says about the nature of society, and the need to act with respect to the professions, is certainly so.

The evidence produced for the Panel, including the dominance of independent schools at the top of the professions, was reviewed in Chapter 6. At the launch of its final report, Britain was termed a 'closed shop society' and the professions were described as becoming more, rather than less, socially exclusive. The report describes aspects of the managed model of reproduction used by middle class parents: what it calls 'opportunity hoarding' (p21) through such practices as work experience (see Chapter 2), and the recruitment of unpaid interns post-graduation. Internship is sometimes seen as essential for being taken on permanently, but these exclusive practices prevent young people from other backgrounds from acquiring the idea that they may enter the professions. They will not have the means.

The Panel recommends action which complements the *New Opportunities* proposals. Some would come under what I have referred to as the first argument for social mobility – widening the social basis for entry to the professions. The Panel's report advocates the abolition of the Connexions service as it does not target students with high aspirations (true – see Chapter 7), and a right of redress in disadvantaged areas, including the right to transfer to a better school. It argues for better and more sustained links between young professionals and students in less advantaged areas, for earlier links with universities and an extra-curricular emphasis on the soft skills of 'communications, teamworking, (and) confidence (building)' (p47), thus enabling the acquisition of the same sort of cultural capital as the middle classes and the professions.

Finally, in this regard, it looks for greater flexibility in the university year to aid recruitment from a wider social basis. We know that new universities are up for this: the paper produced by million+ (2009), the think tank representing 28 new universities, *Social Mobility – Universities Changing Lives* (million+, 2009), was cited in Chapter 6. HESA data, it said, showed a greater proportion of their graduates (17%) were in professional, managerial and technical posts than their parents (8%) three and a half years after graduation. But this continued good news does depend on expansion of the posts in the first place for them to take up.

Significantly, the Fair Access Panel also begins to touch on what I have termed the second argument for social mobility, which is about elite recruitment, as I have called it, or the 'top end' of social mobility as the Sutton Trust term it (2009c). 'There are fewer chances for people to work their way up from the bottom to the top of the professional career ladder', it says (p120), because of what it terms 'job silos that block career paths' due to specialisation, qualification inflation and a 'more risk-averse culture' due to 'increased regulatory and accountability demands'. So, in addition to recommending multiple entry points to professions, and different and flexible ways of working and acquiring qualifications, the Panel recommends that all professions review their current recruitment processes with a view to developing an action plan for improvement by 2010.

As this book went to press, the Government was preparing an implementation plan for this report, but it had not gone public.

Social Justice and the State
Progress to date

So, there has been much far-reaching reform over the past ten years in the UK, with much of it impacting on the central concern of this book – breaking the apparently almost absolute connection between inequality of circumstance and inequality of opportunity. More young people will progress to university from working class backgrounds, being ennobled as I have termed it, but they will continue to require personal qualities above those needed by their independent school peers, and their success will have depended on developed commitment and understanding at all levels of the education service – enhanced professional agency. The social structures enabling middle class succession – what I have termed the managed model of social reproduction – are well-established, working well and unlikely to change as a consequence of anything proposed by current and future governments.

Because of this, success in turning the standards based reform, developments designed to bring on a stream of aspirant working class students to universities, including prestigious ones, require the expansion of professional and managerial employment opportunities if the 'opportunity trap' (Brown, 2006) is to be avoided. This is a clear expectation of government policy, but the best that can be said about the predictions in both New Opportunities and the Fair Access Panel's final report is that they are provisional.

If the expanded opportunities do emerge, however, then it is most likely that the first argument for social mobility will be increasingly satisfied over the next ten years. The professions, and other managerial strata in our society, will begin to acquire a wider social basis than now.

Further progress which is possible

But it is also possible, with further change, that the second argument could begin to be satisfied, with elites becoming less exclusive than now.

For the professions, the action plans recommended by the Fair Access Panel to widen the social basis of their recruitment could be extended to include professional development – which it also touched on – but, most important, fair *promotion*. How will the legal profession, for example, ensure that top judges and barristers will no longer be predominantly from independent schools, and hence restricted social backgrounds, in ten or twenty years' time? This is a further step that needs to be taken.

And prestigious universities could change too. The obstacles to widening access were considered just now, and the steps mentioned could be taken to help overcome them – a change to the examinations system, perhaps allowing something equivalent to the A1, A2 and A3 speculated on by Malcolm. All prestigious universities – by agreement or otherwise – should make revised offers to students from state schools serving working class areas, taking into account the school context, as only some of them do now.

Alternatively, or in addition, the Sutton Trust's most recent proposal (Sutton Trust, 2009a) for prestigious universities could be adopted, whereby they take a quota of local, academically able students from less advantaged communities, initially on a voluntary basis. This would radically change local perceptions of universities often not embedded in their communities. And whatever approach is taken, a broader social basis may later begin to be significant for recruitment to transnational corporations.

However, these further steps would entail a different level of what might be considered interference in the professions' and prestigious universities' independence from any currently proposed. This is not true for examinations authorities, although there may be obstacles there too. And this is the case even if Government began with an invitation to participate in such developments, as they should, perhaps on a pilot basis.

But it would need to be clear that initial non-participation was not sustainable in the medium or long term, as such changes would only begin to even up the dramatic social imbalance in intakes to universities, the professions and to elite recruitment, if they were system wide. This is about social justice; governments should be willing to use the power of the state to help bring it about.

The use of state power in this way would be opposed. Students from working class backgrounds would be competing on the basis of being encouraged and supported by schemes and interventions funded by the taxpayer. And meanwhile, their independent school peers would, according to some, be doing so on their own merits after their parents had bought them a good education with their own money, on top of the taxes they had already paid. And it is easy to imagine the discussion of the gold standard of A Level. So it would be maintained that using the power of the state in these ways would be unfair.

But middle class succession is also about power – this is exactly what opportunity hoarding is. In this book, I have tried to provide snapshots of how such power is exercised, while being represented as meeting the entitlements of children with special qualities. Choice of trajectory is misrecognised as choice of school. So by deciding collectively through elected governments not to use the power of the state, we also tacitly agree to the continuing exercise of power through social structure, and its misrepresentation by false notions of merit. The argument about the small state needs to be seen for what it is.

Should current patterns of reform continue, with the additional pro-posals made here, greater numbers of working class students will emerge over the next twenty years or so from social settings better able to sustain different aspirational identities. They will progress to pres-tigious universities and the leading heights of professions and trans-national elites – the networks identified by Sampson (2004) as pro-ducing the 'establishment'. Because of false notions of merit, however, they may not yet be seen as being there by entitlement, but as the result of special circumstances. And they may see it like this themselves. This further change will take another generation.

Bibliography

AERS (2008) *Research Briefing Paper 5: The Scottish Independent Schools Project.* Available from www.strath.ac.uk accessed 17 September, 2009

AimHigher West Area Partnership (2005) *Opportunities Prospectus – A Guide to the activities available for young people aged 13-30 in the west area partnership.* Available at www.aimhighersw.ac.uk accessed 6 July 2007

AimHigher (2006) *Which Activities are Effective and which are less Effective?* Available from www.aimhigher.ac.uk/practitioner/prgrammes_information/monitoring_ and_evaluation accessed 16 July 2007

Anderson, D, Croudace, C and England A (2005) *Intervention Model (IM) 2005/6 Edition for AimHigher West Partnership.* Bristol: Outreach Centre, University of the West of England

Archer, L (2003 [2006]) The 'Value' of Higher Education in Archer *et al* p119-136

Archer, L, Hutchings and Ross, A (2003) *Higher Education and Social Class – Issues of exclusion and inclusion.* Abingdon: RoutledgeFalmer

Atherton, G, Cymbir, E, Roberts, K, Page, L and Remedios, R (2009) *How Young People Formulate their Views about the Future – Exploratory Research AimHigher.* Central London Partnership, University of Westminster London: DCSF. Available at www.dcsf.gov.uk accessed 3 November 2009

Attwood, R (2008) *Student Support does not go to the neediest, Birkbeck research finds.* London: THE. Available at www.timeshighereducation.co.uk accessed 2 June 2009

Attwood, R (2009) *The Usual Suspects Reign Supreme.* London: THE. Available at www.timeshighereducation.co.uk accessed 8 June 2009

Ball, S (1990) *Politics and Policy Making in Education – Explorations in Policy Sociology.* London: Routledge

Ball, S, Maguire, M and Macrae, S (2000) *Choice, Pathways and Transitions Post-16 – New Youth, new economies in the global city.* London: RoutledgeFarmer

Ball, S (2003a) *Class Strategies and the Education Market – The middle classes and social advantage.* London: RoutledgeFalmer

Ball (2003b) *Social Justice in the Head: Are we all libertarians now?* In Vincent (Ed) (2003)

Ball, S (Ed) (2004) *The RoutledgeFalmer Reader in Sociology of Education.* London: RoutledgeFalmer

Ball, S (2008) *The Education Debate.* Bristol: Policy Press

Beatty, C, Fothergill, S, Gore, T and Powell, R (2007) *The Real Level of Employment 2007.* Sheffield: The Centre for Regional Economic and Social Research, Sheffield Hallam University. Available at www.shu.ac.uk/research/cresr/ accessed 8 July 2009

Beck, U (1986 [1992]) *Risk Society – Towards a New Modernity.* London: Sage

Blanden, J and Machin, S (2007) *Recent Changes in Intergenerational Mobility in Britain.* London: The Sutton Trust. Available at www.suttontrust.com accessed 1 February 2008

Blanden, J, Gregg, P and Machin, S (2005) *Intergenerational Mobility in Europe and North America; A Report supported by the Sutton Trust.* London: LSE. Available at www.lse.ac.uk accessed 20 May 2005

Blanden, J and Machin, S (2007) *Recent Changes in Intergenerational Mobility in Britain.* London: The Sutton Trust. Available at www.suttontrust.com accessed 1 February 2008

Bourdieu, P (1986) *The Forms of Capital.* Reproduced in Ball (2004)

Bourdieu, P and Passeron, J-C (1977) *Reproduction in Education, Society and Culture Second Edition.* London: Sage

Bourdieu, P and Wacquant, J (1992) *An Invitation to Reflexive Sociology.* Cambridge: Polity Press

Boyd, D (2007) *Viewing American class divisions through Facebook and MySpace Apophenia Blog Essay.* 24 June. Available at http://www.danah.org/papers/essays/ClassDivisions.html accessed February 16 2009

Brewer, M, Muriel, A, Phillips, D and Sibieta, L (2008) *Poverty and Inequality in the UK: 2008.* London: The Institute for Fiscal Studies Available at www.ifs.org.uk accessed 5 August 2009

Brighouse, T (2003) Comprehensive Schools then, now and in the future – is it time to draw a line in the sand and create a new ideal? *Forum* 45 (1) p 3-11

Brown, P (2006) The Opportunity Trap in Lauder *et al,* p381-397

Brown, P, Lauder, H and Ashton D (2008) *Education, globalisation and the knowledge economy – A commentary by the Teaching and Learning Research Programme.* London: TLRP. Available at www.tlrp.org accessed 10 March 2009

Brown, P and Lauder, H (2006) Globalisation, Knowledge and the Myth of the Magnet Economy in Lauder *et al,* p317-340

Butler, T and Savage, M (Eds) (1995) *Social Change and the Middle Classes.* London: UCL Press

Butler, T with Robson G (2003) *London Calling: The Middle Classes and the Remaking of Inner London.* Oxford: Berg

Cabinet Office (2008a) *Excellence and Fairness: Achieving world class public services*. London: The Cabinet Office. Available at www.cabinetoffice.gov.uk/strategy/ publications accessed 20 July 2009

Cabinet Office (2008b) *Getting on, getting ahead – A discussion paper: analysing the trends and drivers of social mobility*. London: The Cabinet Office. Available at www.cabinetoffice.gov.uk accessed 12 November 2008.

Cabinet Office/Social Exclusion Taskforce (2008c) *Aspiration and attainment amongst young people in deprived communities: analysis and discussion paper*. London: The Cabinet Office. Available at www.cabinetoffice.gov.uk accessed 7 January 2009

Cabinet Office (2009a) *New Opportunities: Fair Chances for the Future*. Norwich: The Stationery Office. Available at www.cabinetoffice.gov.uk accessed 30 January 2009

Cabinet Office (2009b) *The Panel of Fair Access to the Professions – Phase 1 Report: an analysis of the trends and issues relating to fair access to the Professions*. London: The Cabinet Office. Available at www.cabinetoffice.gov.uk accessed 3 June 2009

Childwise (2009) Monitor Report 2008/9, as reported in the *Guardian*, 19 January 2009. Available at www.guardian.co.uk accessed 16 February 2009

Clarke, P (Ed) (2005) *Improving Schools in Difficulty: Principle and Process*. London: Continuum International

Cremin, H and Thomas, G (2005) Maintaining Underclasses via Contrastive Judgment. *British Journal of Educational Studies* 53 (4) p431-446

CRESR (2005) *New Deal for Communities 2001-2005: An Interim Evaluation*. Sheffield: Sheffield Hallam University 'as part of a contract by the Office of the Deputy Prime Minister'. Available from at http://www.communities.gov.uk accessed 13 August, 2008

Crozier, G, Reay, D, James, D, Jamieson, F, Beedell, P, Hollingworth, S and Williams, K (2008) White Middle Class Parents, identities, educational choice and the urban comprehensive school: dilemmas, ambivalence and moral ambiguity. *British Journal of Sociology of Education* 29 (3) p261-272

Curtis, A, Power, S, Whitty, G, Exley, S and Sasia, A (2008) *Primed for Success? State school entry to prestigious universities*. Paper presented to the annual conference of the British Education Research Association, Heriot-Watt University, Edinburgh, 4 September 2008

DCLG (2008) *Communities in control: real people, real power*. Norwich: The Stationery Office. Available at www.communities.gov.uk accessed 31 July 2009

DCSF (2007) *The Children's Plan – Building brighter futures*. London: The Stationery Office available at www.dcsf.gov.uk accessed 14 January 2008

DCSF (2008a) *Promoting Excellence for All – School Improvement Strategy: raising standards, supporting schools*. Available at www.dcsf.gov.uk/nationalchallenge/ downloads accessed 1 October 2008

DCSF (2008b) *National Challenge – A toolkit for schools and local authorities*. Available at www.dcsf.gov.uk/nationalchallenge/downloads accessed 1 October 2008

DCSF (2008c) *Identifying Gifted and Talented Learners – getting started.* Nottingham: DCSF. Available at http://ygt.dcsf.gov.uk accessed 5 May 2009

DCSF (2008d) *The Extra Mile – How schools succeed in raising aspiration in deprived communities.* Nottingham: DCSF Publications. Available to download at http://publications.teachernet.gov.uk/ accessed 30 July 2009

DCSF (2009) *Your child, your schools, our future: building a 21st century schools system.* London: The Stationery Office. Available at www.dcsf.gov.uk accessed 16 July 2009

DfEE (1999) *Excellence in Cities.* London: The Stationery Office

DfES (2004) *Every Child Matters: Change for Children.* Nottingham: DfESIden

DfES (2005a) *Fair admissions to higher education: recommendations for good practice.* London: DfES

DfES (2005b) *Extended Schools: Access to opportunities and services for all; A Prospectus.* London: DfES

Ecclestone, K, Hughes, M and Biesta, G (Eds) (2009) *Transitions through the Lifecourse.* Abingdon: Routledge

Feinstein, L, Hearn, B and Renton, Z, with Abrahams, C and Macleod, M (Eds) (2007) *Reducing Inequalities: Realising the talents of all.* London: National Children's Bureau

Feldman, S (2008) The curse of the mummies. *Times Higher Education,* 25 September Available at www.timeshighereducation.co.uk accessed February 16 2009

Ferri, E, Bynner, J and Wadsworth, M (2003) *Changing Britain, Changing Lives – Three Generations by the Turn of the Century.* London: Institute of Education

Fitz, J, Edwards, T and Whitty, G (1986) Beneficiaries, Benefits and Costs: An Investigation of the Assisted Places Scheme. *Research Papers in Education* 1 (3)

Foskett, N and Hemsley-Brown (2003) *Economic Aspirations, Cultural Replication and Social Dilemmas – Interpreting the Parental Choice of British Private Schools* In Walford (Ed) p194-207

Foucault, M (1969) *The Archaeology of Knowledge.* London: Routledge

Freeman, J (1998) *Educating the Very Able – Current International Research.* London: The Stationery Office, with the permission of Ofsted

Galinda-Rueda, F, Marcenaro-Gutierrez, O and Vignoles, A (2004) The widening socioeconomic gap in UK Higher Education. *National Institute Economic Review* 190 p75-78

Gewirtz, S (2001) Cloning the Blairs: New Labour's programme for the re-socialisation of working class parents. *Journal of Education Policy* 16 (4) p365-378

Giddens, A (1991) *Modernity and Self-Identity – Self and Society in the Late Modern Age.* Cambridge: Polity Press

Giddens, A (1998) *The Third Way: The Renewal of Social Democracy.* Cambridge: Polity Press

Gilbert, F (2007) *The New School Rules – The parents' guide to getting the best education for your child.* London: Portrait

Gillborn, D and Youdell, D (2000) *Rationing Education – Policy, Practice, Reform and Equity.* Buckingham: the Open University Press

Gilchrist, R, Phillips, D and Ross, A (2003) Participation and potential participation in UK higher education In Archer *et al* p75-96

Gillies, V (2007) *Marginalised Mothers – Exploring working-class experiences of parenting.* Abingdon: Routledge

Gorard, S, with Adnett, N, May, H, Slack, K, Smith, E and Thomas, L (2007) *Overcoming the Barriers to Higher Education.* Stoke-on-Trent: Trentham Books

Granovetter, M (1973) The Strength of Weak Ties. *American Journal of Sociology* 78 (6) p1360-1380

Grenfell, M and James, D with Hodkinson, P, Reay, D and Robbins, D (1998) *Bourdieu and Education – Acts of Practical Theory.* London: Falmer Press

Haberman, M (1991) The Pedagogy of Poverty versus Good Teaching. *Phi Delta Kappan* 73(4) p290-4

Hall, S (1992) The Question of Cultural Identity In Hall *et al* (1992)

Hall, S, Held, D and McGrew, T (Eds) (1992) *Modernity and Its Futures.* Cambridge and Oxford: Polity Press in association with Blackwell's

Halpern, D (2005) *Social Capital.* Cambridge: Polity Press

HMG (2009) Norwich: HMSO. Available at http://www.hmg.gov.uk/workingtogether/download.aspx accessed 24 March 2009

HM Treasury (2006) *Leitch Review of Skills: Prosperity for all the global economy – world class skills, Final Report.* London: HM Treasury, available at www.hm-treasury.gov.uk accessed 4 October 2008

H.M.Treasury (2007) Aiming Higher for young people: a ten year strategy for positive attitudes London: H.M. Treasury. Available at www.hm-treasury.gov.uk accessed 17 January, 2008

Hills, J, Sefton, T and Stewart, K (Eds) (2009) *Towards a More Equal Society? Poverty, inequality and policy since 1997.* Bristol: Policy Press

Howard-Jones, P with Pollard, A, Bakermore, S-J, Rogers, P, Goswami, U, Butterworth, B, Taylor, E, Williamon, A, Morton, J and Kaufman, L (2008) *Neuroscience and Education: Issues and Opportunities – a commentary by the Teaching and Learning Research Programme.* Available from www.tlrp.ac.uk accessed 4 June, 2008

Hutchings, M (2003) Information, advice and cultural discourses of higher education In Archer *et al,* p97-118

James, D and Beedell, P (2009) Transgression for transition? White urban middle class families making and managing 'against the grain' school choices In Ecclestone *et al,* p32-46

Kendall, L, O'Donnell, L, Golden, S, Ridley, K, Machin, S, Rutt, S, McNally, S, Schagen, I, Meghir, C, Stoney, S, Morris, M, West, A and Noden, P (2005) *Excellence in Cities – The National Evaluation of a Policy to Raise Standards in Urban Schools 2000-2003.* London: DfES Available from www.dfes.gsi.gov.uk/ accessed 19 July 2007

Kenway, J and Bullen, E (2008 [2001]) *Consuming Children – education-entertainment+- advertising.* Maidenhead: Open University Press

Lareau, A (2000) *Home Advantage: Social Class and Parental Intervention in Elementary Education.* Maryland: Rowman and Littlefield

Lareau, A (2003) *Unequal Childhoods: Class, Race, and Family Life.* Berkeley, Ca: University of California Press

Lauder, H, Brown, P, Dillabough and Halsey, A (2006) *Education, Globalisation and Social Change.* Oxford: Oxford University Press

Lauder, H, Brown, P, Dillabough and Halsey, A (2006) The Prospects for Education: Individualisation, Globalisation, and Social Change In Lauder *et al* p1-70

Local Government Association/Centre for Social Justice (2009) *Hidden Talents: Re-engaging young people.* London: LGA. Available at www.lga.gov.uk/ accessed 6 July 2009

Lucey, H and Reay, D (2002) Carrying the Beacon of Excellence: social class differentiation and anxiety at a time of transition. *Journal of Education Policy* 17 (3) p321-336

Maddern, K (2009a) New gifted policy to back social mobility. *Times Educational Supplement*, 7th August. Available at www.tes.co.uk accessed 11 August 2009

Maddern, K (2009b) The one in five schools that claims to have no talented pupils could be acting illegally. *Times Educational Supplement*, 23 October. Available at www.tes.co.uk accessed 29 October 2009

Mead, G (1934) *Mind, Self, and Society from the standpoint of a Social Behaviourist.* Chicago: University of Chicago Press

million + (2009) *Social Mobility – Universities Changing Lives.* London: million +. Available at www.millionplus.ac.uk/policy accessed 15 June 2009

Newsam, P (2003) Diversity and admissions to English Secondary Schools. *Forum* 45 (1) p17-18

ODPM (2004) *Tackling Social Exclusion: Taking stock and looking to the future.* London: Office of the Deputy Prime Minister. Available at www.cabinetoffice.gov.uk accessed 31 August 2008

Ofsted (1993) *Access and Achievement in Urban Education.* London: HMSO

Ofsted (2000) *Improving City Schools – Strategies to Promote Educational Inclusion.* London: Ofsted

Ofsted (2009) *Twelve outstanding secondary schools: excelling against the odds.* London: Ofsted. Available at www.ofsted.gov.uk accessed 23 April 2009

Page, B (2006) *Creating a high Aspiration Culture for Young People in the UK.* Ipsos MORI SRI. Available at www.suttontrust.org.uk accessed 2 July 2007

Panel on Fair Access to the Professions (2009) *Unleashing Aspiration: The Final Report of the Panel on Fair Access to the Professions.* London: The Cabinet Office. Available at www.cabinetoffice.gov.uk accessed 22 July 2009

Pollard, A with Filer, A (1996) *The Social World of Children's Learning – Case Studies of Pupils from Four to Seven.* London: Cassell

Pollard, A and Triggs, P (2000) *What Pupils Say – Changing Policy and Practice in Primary Education (Findings from the PACE Project).* London: Continuum

Power, S, Curtis, A, Whitty, G, Edwards, T and Exley, S (2009) *'Embers from the Ashes'? The experience of being an assisted place holder.* London: The Sutton Trust. Available at www.suttontrust.com accessed 19 September, 2009

Power, S, Edwards, T, Whitty, G and Wigfall, V (2003) *Education and the Middle Class.* Buckingham: Open University Press

Power, S, Warren, S, Gillborn, D, Clark, A, Thomas, S and Coate, K (2002) *Education in Deprived Areas – outcomes, inputs and processes.* London: Institute of Education, University of London

Power, S and Whitty, G (2008) *Graduating and gradations within the middle class: the legacy of an elite higher education.* Cardiff: Cardiff University School of Social Sciences. Available at www.cardiff.ac.uk/socsi accessed 1 December 1 2008

Pugsley, L (2003) *Choice or Chance: The University Challenge – How Schools Produce and Reproduce Social Capital in the Choice Process* In *Walford* (Ed) p208-223

Putnam, R (2000) *Bowling Alone – The Collapse and Revival of American Community.* New York: Simon and Schuster

Radnor, H, Koshy, V and Taylor, A (2007) Gifts, Talents and Meritocracy. *Journal of Education Policy* 22 (3) p283-299

Raphael Reed, L, Croudace, C, Harrison, N, Baxter, A and Last, K (2007) *Young Participation in Higher Education: A socio-cultural study of engagement in Bristol South Parliamentary Constituency.* Bristol: University of the West of England

Reay, D, Crozier, G and Clayton, J (2009) 'Strangers in Paradise?': Working Class Students in Elite Universities. *Sociology* 43 (6) p1103-1121

Reay, D, David, M and Ball, S (2005) *Degrees of Choice – social class, race and gender in higher education.* Stoke-on-Trent: Trentham

Reich, R (2001) *Why the rich are getting richer, and the poor, poorer* in Lauder *et al* p308-316.

Riddell, R (2003) *Schools for Our Cities: Urban Learning for the Twenty-First Century.* Stoke-on-Trent: Trentham Books

Riddell, R (2005) Learning Disadvantage and Challenging Schools In Clarke (Ed) p43-55

Riddell, R (2007) Urban Learning and the Need for Varied Urban Curricula and Pedagogies in Pink, W and Noblit, G (Eds) p1027-1048

Riddell (2009) Schools in trouble again: a critique of the National Challenge (2008) *Improving Schools* 12 (1) p71-80

Roberts, K (2001) *Class in Modern Britain.* Basingstoke: Palgrove

Ross, A (2003) Access to higher education: inclusion for the masses? In Archer *et al* p45-74

Sampson, A (2004) *Who Runs This Place? The Anatomy of Britain in the 21st Century.* London: John Murray

Sanderson, I (2006) *Worklessness in Deprived Neighbourhoods: A review of Evidence.* London: Department for Communities and Local Government. Available at www.communities.gov.uk/publications/communities accessed 31 August 2008

Savage, M (2000) *Class Analysis and Social Transformation.* Buckingham: Open University Press

Savage, M, Bagnall, G and Longhurst, B (2005) *Globalisation and Belonging.* London: Sage

Savage, M, Barlow, J, Dickens, P and Fielding, T (1992) *Property, Bureaucracy and Culture: Middle-Class Formation in Contemporary Britain.* London: Routledge

Sefton, T, Hills, J and Sutherland, H (2009) Poverty, inequality and redistribution In Hills *et al* (Eds)

Sennett, R (2006) *The Culture of the New Capitalism.* New Haven: Yale University Press

Sewell, T (1997) *Black Masculinities and Schooling – How Black Boys Survive Modern Schooling.* Stoke-on-Trent: Trentham Books

SHM (2004) *Bristol-Birmingham Schools Comparison Research.* Bristol: Learning and Skills Council

Skeggs, B (2004) *Class, Self, Culture.* London: Routledge

Stewart, K, Sefton, T and Hills, J, (2009) Introduction to Hills *et al* (2009)

Strand, S (2006) *Identifying gifted students: An evaluation of the National Academy for Gifted and Talented Youth (NAGTY) procedure.* Warwick: NAGTY

Sutton Trust (2005) *State School Admissions to our Leading Universities – An Update to 'The Missing 3000'.* London: The Sutton Trust

Sutton Trust (2008) *Increasing higher education participation amongst young people and schools in poor communities (Report to the National Council for Educational Excellence).* London: The Sutton Trust. Available at www.suttontrust.com accessed 30 January 2009

Sutton Trust/Ipsos MORI (2008) *Social Mobility London: the Sutton Trust.* Available at www.suttontrust.com; accessed July 24th 2009

Sutton Trust (2009a) *Innovative University Admissions Worldwide: A Percent Scheme for the UK?* London: the Sutton Trust. Available at www.suttontrust.com accessed July 20 2009

Sutton Trust (2009b) *Attainment Gaps between the most deprived and advantaged schools: a summary and discussion of research by the Education Research Group at the London School of Economics.* London: the Sutton Trust. Available at www.sutton trust.com accessed July 31 2009

Sutton Trust (2009c) *Sutton Trust submission to the House of Commons Children, Schools and Families Committee on Social Mobility and Education and Access to the Professions.* Available at www.suttontrust.com accessed 17 November 2009

Swain, H (2008) *Planning an Open Day Times Higher Education,* 3 January. Available at www.timeshighereducation.co.uk accessed 16 February 2009

Thrupp, M (1999) *Schools Making A Difference: Let's be Realistic – School, Mix, School Effectiveness and the Social Limits of Reform.* Buckingham: Open University Press

Tynan, B (2008) *Make Your Child Brilliant – Uncovering your child's hidden gifts.* London: Quadrille

Universities UK (2003) *Fair Enough? Wider access to university by identifying potential to succeed.* London: Universities UK. Available from www.universitiesuk. ac.uk/Publications accessed 2 June 2009

Vincent, C (Ed) (2003) *Social Justice, Education and Identity.* London: Routledge Farmer

Vincent, C and Ball, S (2006) *Childcare, Choice and Class Practices – Middle-Class Parents and Their Children.* Abingdon: Routledge

Walford, G (Ed) (2003) *British Private Schools – Research on Policy and Practice.* London: Woburn Press

Watts, M and Bridges, D (2006) The Value of Non-participation in higher education. *Journal of Education Policy* 21 (3) p 267-290

West, A and Noden, P (2003) *Parental Choice and Involvement: Private and State Schools in Walford* (Ed) p177-193

Wilce, H (2004) *Help Your Child Succeed at School.* London: Piatkus

Willis, P (1977) *Learning to Labour: How Working Class get Working Class Jobs.* New York: Columbia University Press (Morningside Edition)

Wolf, A (2002) *Does Education Matter? Myths about education and economic growth.* London: Penguin Group

Woods, L, Makepeace, G, Joshi, H and Dolton, P (2003) *The World of Paid Work* In Ferri *et al*, p71-104

Index